I0018762

SUSE Linux Enterprise Server 12 - AutoYaST

A catalogue record for this book is available from the Hong Kong Public Libraries.

Published in Hong Kong by Samurai Media Limited.

Email: info@samuraimedia.org

ISBN 978-988-8406-55-5

Contents

1 Introduction

AutoYaST is a system for installing one or more SUSE Linux Enterprise systems automatically and without user intervention. AutoYaST installations are performed using an AutoYaST control file (also called “profile”) with installation and configuration data. That control file can be created using the configuration interface of AutoYaST and can be provided to YaST during installation in different ways.

1.1 Motivation

In an article in issue 78, the Linux Journal (http://www.linuxjournal.com/) writes:

“ A standard Linux installation asks many questions about what to install, what hardware to configure, how to configure the network interface, etc. Answering these questions once is informative and maybe even fun. But imagine a system engineer who needs to set up a new Linux network with many machines. Now, the same issues need to be addressed and the same questions answered repeatedly. This makes the task very inefficient, not to mention a source of irritation and boredom. Hence, a need arises to automate this parameter and option selection.”

“The thought of simply copying the hard disks naturally crosses one's mind. This can be done quickly, and all the necessary functions and software will be copied without option selection. However, the fact is that simple copying of hard disks causes the individual computers to become too similar. This, in turn, creates an altogether new mission of having to reconfigure the individual settings on each PC. For example, IP addresses for each machine will need to be reset. If this is not done properly, strange and inexplicable behavior results.”

A regular installation of SUSE Linux Enterprise is semi-automated by default. The user is requested to select the necessary information at the beginning of the installation (usually language only), YaST then generates a proposal for the underlying system depending on different factors and system parameters. Usually—and especially for new systems—such a proposal can be used to install the system and provides a usable installation. The steps following the proposal are fully automated.

AutoYaST can be used where no user intervention is required or where customization is required. Using an AutoYaST control file, YaST prepares the system for a custom installation and avoids any interaction with the user, unless specified in the file controlling the installation.

AutoYaST is not an automated GUI system. This means that usually many screens will be skipped —you will never see the language selection interface, for example. AutoYaST will simply pass the language parameter to the sub-system without displaying any language related interface.

1.2 Overview and Concept

Using AutoYaST, multiple systems can easily be installed in parallel and quickly. They need to share the same environment and similar, but not necessarily identical, hardware. The installation is defined by an XML configuration file (usually named `autoinst.xml`) called the "AutoYaST control file". It can initially be created using existing configuration resources easily be tailored for any specific environment.

AutoYaST is fully integrated and provides various options for installing and configuring a system. The main advantage over other auto-installation systems is the possibility to configure a computer by using existing modules and avoiding using custom scripts which are normally executed at the end of the installation.

This document will guide you through the three steps of auto-installation:

- Preparation: All relevant information about the target system is collected and turned into the appropriate directives of the control file. The control file is transferred onto the target system where its directives will be parsed and fed into YaST.
- Installation: YaST performs the installation of the basic system using the data from the AutoYaST control file.
- Configuration: After the installation of the basic system, the system configuration is performed in the second stage of the installation. User defined post-installation scripts from the AutoYaST control file will also be executed at this stage.

Note: Second Stage

A regular installation of SUSE Linux Enterprise Server 12 SP1 is performed in a single stage. The auto-installation process, however, is divided into two stages. After the installation of the basic system the system boots into the second stage where the system configuration is done.

The second stage can be turned off with the `second_stage` parameter:

```
<general>
```

```
  <mode>
    <confirm config:type="boolean">false</confirm>
    <second_stage config:type="boolean">false</second_stage>
  </mode>
</general>
```

The complete and detailed process is illustrated in the following figure:

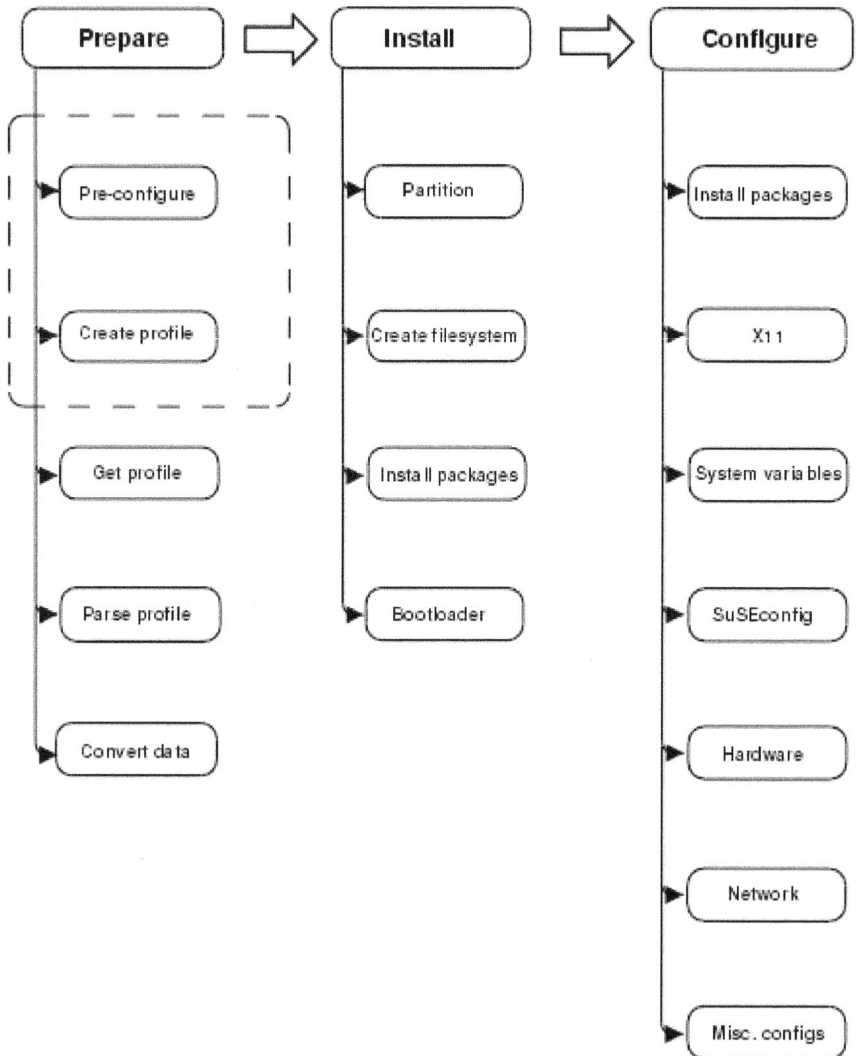

FIGURE 1.1: AUTO-INSTALLATION PROCESS

2 The Control File

2.1 Introduction

The control file usually is a configuration description for a single system. It consists of sets of resources with properties including support for complex structures such as lists, records, trees and large embedded or referenced objects.

Important: Control Files from Previous Releases are Incompatible

A lot of major changes were introduced with SUSE Linux Enterprise Server 12 (the switch to systemd and GRUB 2 for example). These changes also required fundamental changes in AutoYaST, therefore you cannot use AutoYaST control files created on previous SUSE Linux Enterprise versions to install SUSE Linux Enterprise Server 12 and vice versa.

2.2 Format

The XML configuration format provides a consistent file structure, which is easy to learn and to remember when attempting to configure a new system.

The AutoYaST control file uses XML to describe the system installation and configuration. XML is a commonly used mark up and many users are familiar with the concepts of the language and the tools used to process XML files. If you edit an existing control file or create a control file using an editor from scratch, it is strongly recommended to validate the control file using a validating XML parser such as `xmllint`, for example.

The following example shows a control file in XML format:

EXAMPLE 2.1: AUTOYAST CONTROL FILE (PROFILE)

```
<?xml version="1.0"?>
<!DOCTYPE profile>
<profile
  xmlns="http://www.suse.com/1.0/yast2ns"
  xmlns:config="http://www.suse.com/1.0/configns">
  <partitioning  config:type="list">
```

```
    <drive>
      <device>/dev/sda</device>
      <partitions config:type="list">
        <partition>
          <filesystem config:type="symbol">btrfs</filesystem>
          <size>10G</size>
          <mount>/</mount>
        </partition>
        <partition>
          <filesystem config:type="symbol">xfs</filesystem>
          <size>120G</size>
          <mount>/data</mount>
        </partition>
      </partitions>
    </drive>
  </partitioning>
  <scripts>
    <pre-scripts>
      <script>
        <interpreter>shell</interpreter>
        <filename>start.sh</filename>
        <source>
        <![CDATA[
#!/bin/sh
echo "Starting installation"
exit 0

]]>

        </source>
      </script>
    </pre-scripts>
  </scripts>
</profile>
```

2.3 Structure

Below is an example of a basic control file container, the actual content of which is explained later on in this chapter.

EXAMPLE 2.2: CONTROL FILE CONTAINER

```
<?xml version="1.0"?>
<!DOCTYPE profile>
<profile
  xmlns="http://www.suse.com/1.0/yast2ns"
  xmlns:config="http://www.suse.com/1.0/configns">
  <!-- RESOURCES -->
</profile>
```

The `<profile>` element (root node) contains one or more distinct resource elements. The permissible resource elements are specified in the schema files

2.3.1 Resources and Properties

A resource element either contains multiple and distinct property and resource elements, or multiple instances of the same resource element, or it is empty. The permissible content of a resource element is specified in the schema files.

A property element is either empty or contains a literal value. The permissible property elements and values in each resource element are specified in the schema files

An element can be either a container of other elements (a resource) or it has a literal value (a property); it can never be both. This restriction is specified in the schema files. A configuration component with more than one value must either be represented as some kind of embedded list in a property value or as a nested resource.

2.3.2 Nested Resources

Nested resource elements allow a tree-like structure of configuration components to be built to any level.

EXAMPLE 2.3: NESTED RESOURCES

```
...
<drive>
  <device>/dev/sda</device>
  <partitions> <!-- this is wrong, explanation below -->
    <partition>
      <size>10G</size>
      <mount>/</mount>
    </partition>
    <partition>
      <size>1G</size>
      <mount>/tmp</mount>
    </partition>
  </partitions>
</drive>
....
```

In the example above the disk resource consists of a device property and a partitions resource. The partitions resource contains multiple instances of the partition resource. Each partition resource contains a size and mount property.

The XML schema defines the partitions element as a resource supporting one or multiple partition element children. If only one partition resource is specified it is important to use the `config:type` attribute of the partitions element to indicate that the content is a resource, in this case a list. Using the partitions element with out specifying the type in this case will result in undefined behavior as YaST will improperly interpret the partitions resource as a property. The example below illustrates this use case.

EXAMPLE 2.4: NESTED RESOURCES WITH TYPE ATTRIBUTES

```
...
<drive>
  <device>/dev/sda</device>
  <partitions config:type="list">
     <partition>
        <size>10G</size>
        <mount>/</mount>
```

```
    </partition>
    <partition>
      <size>1G</size>
      <mount>/tmp</mount>
    </partition>
  </partitions>
</drive>
....
```

2.3.3 Attributes

Global attributes are used to define metadata on resources and properties. Attributes are used to define context switching. They are also used for naming and typing properties as shown in the previous sections. Attributes are in a separate namespace so they do not need to be treated as reserved words in the default namespace.

Global attributes are defined in the configuration namespace and must always be prefixed with `config:` . All attributes are optional. Most can be used with both resource and property elements but some can only be used with one type of element which is specified in the schema files.

The type of an element is defined using the `config:type` attribute. The type of a resource element is always RESOURCE, although this can also be made explicit with this attribute (to ensure correct identification of an empty element, for example, when there is no schema file to refer to). A resource element cannot be any other type and this restriction is specified in the schema file. The type of a property element determines the interpretation of its literal value. The type of a property element defaults to `STRING`, as specified in the schema file. The full set of permissible types is specified in the schema file.

2.4 RELAX NG—A Schema Language for XML

A RELAX NG schema specifies a pattern for the structure and content of an XML document. A RELAX NG schema thus identifies a class of XML documents consisting of those documents that match the pattern. A RELAX NG schema is itself an XML document.

3 Creating A Control File

3.1 Collecting Information

To create the control file, you need to collect information about the systems your are going to install. This includes hardware data and network information among other things. Make sure you have the following information about the machines you want to install:

- Hard disk types and sizes
- Graphical interface and attached monitor, if any
- Network interface and MAC address if known (for example, when using DHCP)

3.2 Using the Configuration Management System (CMS)

To create the control file for one or more computers, a configuration interface based on YaST is provided. This system depends on existing modules which are usually used to configure a computer in regular operation mode, for example, after SUSE Linux Enterprise Server is installed.

The configuration management system lets you create control files easily and lets you manage a repository of configurations for the use in a networked environment with multiple clients.

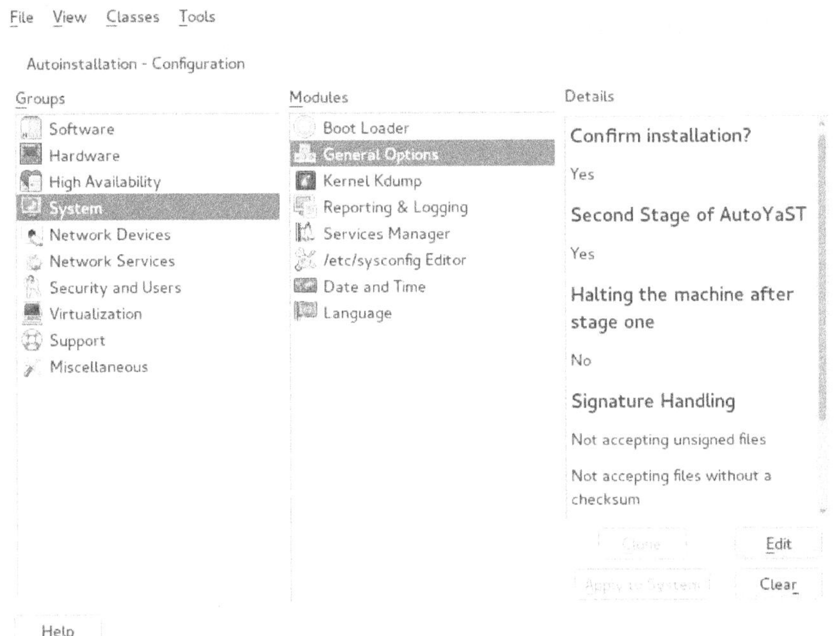

FIGURE 3.1: CONFIGURATION SYSTEM

3.2.1 Creating a New Control File

With some exceptions, almost all resources of the control file can be configured using the configuration management system. The system offers flexibility and the configuration of some resources is identical to the one available in the YaST control center. In addition to the existing and familiar modules new interfaces were created for special and complex configurations, for example for partitioning, general options and software.

Furthermore, using a CMS guarantees the validity of the resulting control file and its direct use for starting automated installation.

Make sure the configuration system is installed (package `autoyast2` and call it using the YaST control center or as root with the following command (make sure the `DISPLAY` variable is set correctly to start the graphical user interface instead of the text based one):

```
/sbin/yast2 autoyast
```

3.3 Creating/Editing a Control File Manually

If editing the control file manually, make sure it has a valid syntax. To check the syntax, use the tools already available on the distribution. For example, to verify that the file is well-formed, use the utility **xmllint** available with the `libxml2` package:

```
xmllint <control file>
```

If the control file is not well formed, for example, if a tag is not closed, **xmllint** will report about the errors.

Before going on with the autoinstallation, fix any errors resulting from such checks. The autoinstallation process cannot be started with an invalid and not well-formed control file.

You can use any XML editor available on your system or any text editor with XML support (for example, Emacs, Vim). However, it is not optimal to create the control file manually for many machines and it should only be seen as an interface between the autoinstallation engine and the Configuration Management System (CMS).

Tip: Using Emacs as an XML Editor

The built-in nxml-mode turns Emacs into a fully-fledged XML editor with automatic tag completion and validation. Refer to the Emacs help for instructions on how to set up nxml-mode.

3.4 Creating a Control File via Script with XSLT

If you have a template and want to change a few things via script or command line, use an XSLT processor like `xsltproc`. For example, if you have an AutoYaST control file and want to fill out the host name via script for any reason (if doing this so often, you want to script it)

First, create an XSL file

EXAMPLE 3.1: EXAMPLE FILE FOR REPLACING THE HOST NAME/DOMAIN BY SCRIPT

```
<?xml version="1.0" encoding="utf-8"?>
<xsl:stylesheet xmlns:xsl="http://www.w3.org/1999/XSL/Transform"
  xmlns:y2="http://www.suse.com/1.0/yast2ns"
```

```
  xmlns:config="http://www.suse.com/1.0/configns"
  xmlns="http://www.suse.com/1.0/yast2ns"
  version="1.0">
  <xsl:output method="xml" encoding="UTF-8" indent="yes" omit-xml-declaration="no"
 cdata-section-elements="source"/>

  <!-- the parameter names -->
  <xsl:param name="hostname"/>
  <xsl:param name="domain"/>

  <xsl:template match="/">
    <xsl:apply-templates select="@*|node()"/>
  </xsl:template>

  <xsl:template match="y2:dns">
    <xsl:copy>
      <!-- where to copy the parameters -->
      <domain><xsl:value-of select="string($domain)"/></domain>
      <hostname><xsl:value-of select="string($hostname)"/></hostname>
      <xsl:apply-templates select="@*|node()"/>
    </xsl:copy>
  </xsl:template>


  <xsl:template match="@*|node()" >
    <xsl:copy>
      <xsl:apply-templates select="@*|node()"/>
    </xsl:copy>
  </xsl:template>

</xsl:stylesheet>
```

This file expects the host name and the domain name as parameters from the user.

```
<xsl:param name="hostname"/>
<xsl:param name="domain"/>
```

There will be a copy of those parameters in the dns section of the control file. That means, if there already is a domain element in the dns section, you will get a second one (no good).

For more information about XSLT, go to the official Web page www.w3.org/TR/xslt [http://www.w3.org/TR/xslt]

4 Configuration and Installation Options

This chapter introduces important parts of a control file for standard purposes. To learn about other available options, use the configuration management system.

Note that for some configuration options to work, additional packages need to be installed, depending on the software selection you have configured. If you choose to install a minimal system then some packages might be missing and need to be added to the individual package selection.

YaST will install packages required in the second phase of the installation and before the post-installation phase of AutoYaST has started. However, if necessary YaST modules are not available in the system, important configuration steps will be skipped. For example, no security settings will be configured if `yast2-security` is not installed.

4.1 General Options

General options include all the settings related to the installation process and the environment of the installed system.

The mode section configures the behavior of AutoYaST with regard to confirmation and rebooting. The following needs to be in the <general> <mode> section.

By default, the user must confirm the auto-installation process. This option allows the user to view and change the settings for a target system before they are committed and can be used for debugging. `confirm` is set to `true` by default to avoid recursive installs when the system schedules a reboot after initial system setup. Only disable confirmation if you want to carry out a fully unattended installation.

With `halt` you cause AutoYaST to shut down the machine after all packages have been installed. Instead of a reboot into stage two, the machine is turned off. The boot loader is already installed and all your chroot scripts have run.

`final_halt` and `final_reboot` halts or reboots the machine after the installation and the configuration are finished at the end of stage 2.

`final_restart_services`: After installation and configuration are finished at the end of stage 2 all services will be restarted by default. With this flag set to `false` no restart will be done.

`activate_systemd_default_target`: After installation and configuration are finished at the end of stage 2 the default target system will be activated.

`ntp_sync_time_before_installation` specifies the NTP server with which the system time has to be synchronized before starting the installation on the target system. It will be not synchronized if this flag has not been used. Please keep in mind that you need a reachable NTP server and network connections while running the installation.

`max_systemd_wait` specifies how long AutoYaST waits at most for systemd to set up the default target. Normally you do not need to bother with this entry. If it is not preset a reasonable default (30 seconds) is used.

Attribute	Values	Description
`confirm`	If this boolean is set to `true`, the installation stops at the confirmation screen (also called proposal screen) and needs to be confirmed with the *Install* button. `<confirm config:type="boolean">true</confirm>`	Optional. The default is true.
`halt`	Shuts down the machine after the first stage. So if you turn it on again, the machine boots and the second stage of the autoinstallation starts. `<halt config:type="boolean">true</halt>`	Optional. The default is false.
`second_stage`	This boolean determines if AutoYaST will run in the second stage too (after the partitioning, software and boot loader installation of the	Optional. The default is true.

Attribute	Values	Description
	first stage). If you set this to `false`, a normal manual installation happens in the second stage. `<second_stage config:type="boolean">true</second_stage>`	
`final_reboot`	If you set this to `true`, the machine will reboot at the very end of the installation (when everything is installed and configured at the end of the second stage). `<final_reboot config:type="boolean">true</final_reboot>`	Optional. The default is `false`. It makes no sense to set this and `final_halt` to `true`.
`final_halt`	If you set this to `true`, the machine will shut down at the very end of the installation (when everything is installed and configured at the end of the second stage). `<final_halt config:type="boolean">true</final_halt>`	Optional. The default is `false`. It makes no sense to set this and `final_reboot` to `true`.
`final_restart_services`	If you set this entry to `false`, all services will *not* be restarted at the very end of the installation (when	Optional. The default is `true`.

Attribute	Values	Description
	everything is installed and configured at the end of the second stage). `<final_restart_services config:type="boolean">false</final_restart_services>`	
`activate_systemd_default_target`	If you set this entry to `false`, the default target will not be activated via the call **`systemctl isolate`**. `<activate_systemd_default_target config:type="boolean">false</activate_systemd_default_target>`	Optional. The default is `true`.

AutoYaST allows you to configure the proposal screen with the <proposals config:type="list"> option in the control file. All proposals that are listed in that section are shown in the proposal screen if you set the `confirm` option to `true`. Proposals are also used during the regular installation and can be found in the file `control.xml` in the root directory of the installation media.

EXAMPLE 4.1: GENERAL OPTIONS

```
<general>
  <signature-handling>
    <accept_unsigned_file config:type="boolean">true</accept_unsigned_file>
    <accept_file_without_checksum config:type="boolean">true</
accept_file_without_checksum>
    <accept_verification_failed config:type="boolean">true</
accept_verification_failed>
    <accept_unknown_gpg_key config:type="boolean">true</accept_unknown_gpg_key>
    <import_gpg_key config:type="boolean">true</import_gpg_key>
    <accept_non_trusted_gpg_key config:type="boolean">true</
accept_non_trusted_gpg_key>
    </signature-handling>
```

```
    <cio_ignore config:type="boolean">false</cio_ignore>       <! -- IBM System z
only -->
  <mode>
    <halt config:type="boolean">false</halt>
    <forceboot config:type="boolean">false</forceboot>
    <final_reboot config:type="boolean">false</final_reboot>
    <final_halt config:type="boolean">false</final_halt>
    <confirm config:type="boolean">true</confirm>
    <second_stage config:type="boolean">true</second_stage>
  </mode>
  <proposals config:type="list">
    <proposal>partitions_proposal</proposal>
  </proposals>
  <wait>
    <pre-modules config:type="list">
      <module>
        <name>networking</name>
        <sleep>
          <time config:type="integer">10</time>
          <feedback config:type="boolean">true</feedback>
        </sleep>
        <script>
          <source>sleep 5</source>
          <debug config:type="boolean">false</debug>
        </script>
      </module>
    </pre-modules>
    <post-modules config:type="list">
      <module>
        <name>networking</name>
        <sleep>
          <time config:type="integer">3</time>
          <feedback config:type="boolean">true</feedback>
        </sleep>
        <script>
          <source>sleep 7</source>
```

```
      <debug config:type="boolean">false</debug>
    </script>
  </module>
 </post-modules>
</wait>
<storage>
 <!--
    partition_alignment:
      align_optimal  - That's the default. Partitions are aligned like the
                       kernel suggests. This can lead to problem with some
                       machines/bioses that are unable to boot with that
                       alignment
      align_cylinder -  Partitions always start on a cylinder boundary
 -->
  <partition_alignment config:type="symbol">align_cylinder</partition_alignment>
</storage>
</general>
```

You can let AutoYaST **sleep** before and after each module run during the second stage. You can run scripts and/or pass a value (in seconds) for AutoYaST to sleep. In the example above AutoYaST will sleep for 15 seconds (10+5) before the network configuration starts and 10 seconds (3+7) after the network configuration is done. The scripts in the example do not really make a lot of sense because you could pass that value as “time” value too. They are only used to show how scripts in the wait section work now.

With the flag `cio_ignore` devices can be blacklisted. This option is available on IBM System z *only*.

Tip: Enabling Multipath for the Installation

When installing on a network storage that is accessed via multiple paths, you need to enable multipath for the installation with the `start_multipath` parameter that needs to be placed within the following XML structure:

```
<general>
  <storage>
    <start_multipath config:type="boolean">true</start_multipath>
  </storage>
```

```
</general>
```

Alternatively, you can pass the following parameter to linuxrc: `LIBSTORAGE_MULTIPATH_AUTOSTART=ON`

4.2 Reporting

The `report` resource manages three types of pop-ups that may appear during installation:

- message pop-ups (usually non-critical, informative messages),
- warning pop-ups (if something might go wrong),
- error pop-ups (in case an error occurs).

EXAMPLE 4.2: REPORTING BEHAVIOR

```
<report>
  <messages>
    <show config:type="boolean">true</show>
    <timeout config:type="integer">10</timeout>
    <log config:type="boolean">true</log>
  </messages>
  <errors>
    <show config:type="boolean">true</show>
    <timeout config:type="integer">10</timeout>
    <log config:type="boolean">true</log>
  </errors>
  <warnings>
    <show config:type="boolean">true</show>
    <timeout config:type="integer">10</timeout>
    <log config:type="boolean">true</log>
  </warnings>
</report>
```

Depending on your experience, you can skip, log and show (with timeout) those messages. It is recommended to show all `messages` with timeout. Warnings can be skipped in some places but should not be ignored.

The default setting in auto-installation mode is to show all messages without logging and without timeout.

Warning: Critical System Messages

Note that not all messages during installation are controlled by the `report` resource. Some critical messages concerning package installation and partitioning will show up ignoring your settings in the `report` section. Usually those messages will need to be answered with *Yes* or *No*.

4.3 System Registration and Extension Selection

Registering the system with the can be configured within the `suse_register` resource. The following example registers the system with the SUSE Customer Center. In case your organization provides its own registration server, you need to specify the required data with the `reg_server*` properties. Refer to the table below for details.

```
<suse_register>
  <do_registration config:type="boolean">true</do_registration>
  <email>tux@example.com</email>
  <reg_code>MY_SECRET_REGCODE</reg_code>
  <install_updates config:type="boolean">true</install_updates>
  <slp_discovery config:type="boolean">false</slp_discovery>
</suse_register>
```

As an alternative to the fully automated registration, AutoYaST can also be configured to start the YaST registration module during the installation. this offers the possibility to enter the registration data manually. The following XML code is required:

```
<general>
 <semi-automatic config:type="list">
   <semi-automatic_entry>scc</semi-automatic_entry>
 </semi-automatic>
</general>
```

Tip: Using the Installation Network Settings

In case you need to use the same network settings that were used for the installation, AutoYaST needs to run the network setup in stage 1 right before the registration is started:

```
<networking>
  <setup_before_proposal config:type="boolean">true</setup_before_proposal
</networking>
```

TABLE 4.1: SYSTEM REGISTRATION: XML REPRESENTATION

Element	Description	Comment
`do_registration`	Specify whether the system should be registered or not. Can be set to `true` or `false`. `<do_registration config:type="boolean" >true</do_registration>`	If set to `false` all other options are ignored and the system is not registered.
`e-mail`	The e-mail address matching the registration code. `<email>tux@example.com</email>`	Required value.
`reg_code`	The registration code. `<reg_code>SECRET_REGCODE</reg_code>`	Required value.
`install_updates`	Defines if the update repositories provided by the registration server are used during the installation (`true`) or not (`false`). `<install_updates config:type="boolean" >true</install_updates>`	Optional. The default value is `false`.
`slp_discovery`	Search for the registration server via SLP.	Optional. The default value is `false`.

Element	Description	Comment
	`<slp_discovery config:type="boolean">true</slp_discovery>`	Expects to find a single server. If more than one server is found, the installation will fail. In case there is more than one registration server available, you need to specify one with `reg_server`. Optional, If neither `slp_discovery` or `reg_server` are set, the system is registered with the SUSE Customer Center.

`reg_server`	URl to the SMT server
	`<reg_server>`
	`https://smt.example.com`
	`</reg_server>`
		Optional, If neither `slp_discovery` or `reg_server` are set, the system is registered with the SUSE Customer Center.

`reg_server_cert_fingerprint_type`	Fingerprint type. Can either be `SHA1` or `SHA256`.
	`<reg_server_cert_fingerprint_type>`
	`SHA1`
	`</reg_server_cert_fingerprint_type>`
		Requires a checksum value provided with `reg_server_cert_fingerprint`. Using the fingerprint is recommended, since it ensures the SSL certificate is verified. The matching certificate will be automatically imported when the SSL communication fails because of a verification error.

`reg_server_cert_fingerprint`	Fingerprint value in hexadecimal notion (case-insensitive). `<reg_server_cert_fingerprint>`	Requires a fingerprint type value provided with `reg_server_cert_fingerprint_type`. Using the fingerprint is rec-

Element	Description	Comment
	`01:AB...:EF` `</reg_server_cert_fingerprint>`	ommended, since it ensures the SSL certificate is verified. The matching certificate will be automatically imported when the SSL communication fails because of a verification error.

`reg_server_cert`	Path to the SSL certificate on the server.
	`<reg_server_cert>`
	`  http://smt.example.com/smt.crt`
	`</reg_server_cert>`
		Using this option is not recommended, since the certificate that is downloaded is not verified. Use `reg_server_cert_fingerprint` instead.

`addons`	Specify an extension from the registration server that should be added to the installation repositories. See Section 4.3.1, "Extensions" for details.	

4.3.1 Extensions

The SUSE Customer Center provides several extensions, such as sle-sdk (Software Development Kit - SDK) that can be added as additional installation sources during the installation. Adding extensions can be configured via the `addons` property within the `suse_register` block. Below is a list of all extensions available for SUSE Linux Enterprise on x86_64:

Note: Availability of Extensions

The availability of extensions is product and architecture dependent. All listed extensions are available for SUSE Linux Enterprise Server on the x86_64 architecture. Not all extensions are available on other architectures. The only extension available for SUSE Linux Enterprise Desktop is the sle-sdk.

Some extensions, such as the sle-we, sle-ha and sle-ha-geo require a registration code.

```
<addons config:type="list">
  <addon>
    <arch>x86_64</arch>
    <name>sle-ha</name>
    <reg_code>YOUR_REG_CODE_HERE</reg_code>
    <release_type>nil</release_type>
    <version>12</version>
  </addon>
  <addon>
    <arch>x86_64</arch>
    <name>sle-ha-geo</name>
    <reg_code>YOUR_REG_CODE_HERE</reg_code>
    <release_type>nil</release_type>
    <version>12</version>
  </addon>
  <addon>
    <arch>x86_64</arch>
    <name>sle-module-web-scripting</name>
    <reg_code/>
    <release_type>nil</release_type>
    <version>12</version>
  </addon>
  <addon>
    <arch>x86_64</arch>
    <name>sle-module-adv-systems-management</name>
    <reg_code/>
    <release_type>nil</release_type>
    <version>12</version>
  </addon>
  <addon>
    <arch>x86_64</arch>
    <name>sle-module-legacy</name>
    <reg_code/>
    <release_type>nil</release_type>
    <version>12</version>
```

```
  </addon>
  <addon>
    <arch>x86_64</arch>
    <name>sle-we</name>
    <reg_code>YOUR_REG_CODE_HERE</reg_code>
    <release_type>nil</release_type>
    <version>12</version>
  </addon>
  <addon>
    <arch>x86_64</arch>
    <name>sle-sdk</name>
    <reg_code/>
    <release_type>nil</release_type>
    <version>12</version>
  </addon>
  <addon>
    <arch>x86_64</arch>
    <name>sle-module-public-cloud</name>
    <reg_code/>
    <release_type>nil</release_type>
    <version>12</version>
  </addon>
</addons>
```

4.4 The Boot Loader

This documentation is for **yast2-bootloader** and applies to SLE 12 SP1. For older product versions, use the documentation that comes with your distribution in /usr/share/doc/packages/autoyast2/

The general structure of the AutoYaST boot loader part looks like the following:

```
<bootloader>
  <loader_type>
    <!-- boot loader type (grub2 or grub2-efi) -->
  </loader_type>
```

```
  <global>
    <!--
      entries defining the installation settings for GRUB 2 and
      the generic boot code
    -->
  </global>
  <device_map config:type="list">
    <!-- entries defining the order of devices -->
  </device_map>
</bootloader>
```

4.4.1 Loader Type

Define which boot loader to use: `grub2` or `grub2-efi`.

```
<loader_type>grub2</loader_type>
```

4.4.2 Globals

This is an important if optional part. Define here where to install GRUB 2 and how the boot process will work. Again, **`yast2-bootloader`** proposes a configuration if you do not define one. Usually the AutoYaST control file includes only this part and all other parts are added automatically during installation by **`yast2-bootloader`**. Unless you have some special requirements, do not specify the boot loader configuration in the XML file.

```
<global>
  <activate config:type="boolean">true</activate>
  <timeout config:type="integer">10</timeout>
  <suse_btrfs config:type="boolean">true</suse_btrfs>
  <terminal>gfxterm</terminal>
  <gfxmode>1280x1024x24</gfxmode>
</global>
```

Attribute	Description
activate	Set the boot flag on the boot partition. The boot partition can be / if there is no separate /boot partition. If the boot partition is on a logical partition, the boot flag is set to the extended partition. <activate config:type="boolean">true</activate>
append	Kernel parameters added at the end of boot entries for normal and recovery mode. <append>nomodeset vga=0x317</append>
boot_boot	Write GRUB 2 to a separate /boot partition. If no separate /boot partition exists, GRUB 2 will be written to / . <boot_boot>false</boot_boot>
boot_custom	Write GRUB 2 to a custom device. <boot_custom>/dev/sda3</boot_custom>
boot_extended	Write GRUB 2 to the extended partition (important if you want to use a generic boot code and the /boot partition is logical). NOTE: if the boot partition is logical, you should use boot_mbr (write GRUB 2 to MBR) rather than generic_mbr . <boot_extended>false</boot_extended>
boot_mbr	Write GRUB 2 to MBR of the first disk in the order (device.map includes order of disks).

Attribute	Description
	`<boot_mbr>false</boot_mbr>`
`boot_root`	Write GRUB 2 to `/` partition. `<boot_root>false</boot_root>`
`generic_mbr`	Write generic boot code to MBR, will be ignored if boot_mbr is set to `true`. `<generic_mbr config:type="boolean">false</generic_mbr>`
`gfxmode`	Graphical resolution of the GRUB 2 screen (requires <terminal> to be set to `gfxterm`. Valid entries are `auto`, *`HORIZONTALxVERTICAL`*, or *`HORIZONTALxVERTICALxCOLOR DEPTH`*. You can display the screen resolutions available to GRUB 2 on a particular system by typing **`vbeinfo`** at the GRUB 2 command line in the running system. `<gfxmode>1280x1024x24</gfxmode>`
`os_prober`	If set to `true`, automatically searches for operating systems already installed and generates boot entries for them during the installation `<os_prober config:type="boolean">false</os_prober>`
`suse_btrfs`	If set to `true`, booting from Btrfs snapshots will be enabled.

Attribute	Description
	`<suse_btrfs config:type="boolean">false</suse_btrfs>`
`serial`	Command to execute if the GRUB 2 terminal mode is set to `serial`. `<serial> serial --speed=115200 --unit=0 --word=8 --parity=no --stop=1 </serials>`
`terminal`	Specify the GRUB 2 terminal mode to use, Valid entries are `console`, `gfxterm`, and `serial`. If set to `serial`, the serial command needs to be specified with <serial>, too. `<terminal>serial</terminal>`
`timeout`	The timeout in seconds until the default boot entry is booted automatically. `<timeout config:type="integer">10</timeout>`
`vgamode`	Adds the Kernel parameter `vga=VALUE` to the boot entries. `<vgamode>0x317</vgamode>`
`xen-append`	Kernel parameters added at the end of boot entries for Xen guests. `<append>nomodeset vga=0x317</append>`

Attribute	Description
`xen-kernel-append`	Kernel parameters added at the end of boot entries for Xen kernels on the VM Host Server. `<xen-append>dom0_mem=768M</xen-append>`

4.4.3 Device map

GRUB 2 avoids mapping problems between BIOS drives and Linux devices by using device ID strings (UUIDs) or file system labels when generating its configuration files. GRUB 2 utilities create a temporary device map on the fly, which is usually sufficient, particularly on single-disk systems. However, if you need to override the automatic device mapping mechanism, create your custom mapping in this section.

```
<device_map config:type="list">
  <device_map_entry>
    <firmware>hd0</firmware> <!-- order of devices in target map  -->
    <linux>/dev/disk/by-id/ata-ST3500418AS_6VM23FX0</linux> <!-- name of device
 (disk)  -->
  </device_map_entry>
</device_map>
```

4.5 Partitioning

4.5.1 Drive Configuration

The elements listed below must be placed within the following XML structure:

```
<profile>
  <partitioning config:type="list">
    <drive>
```

```
    ...
  </drive>
 </partitioning>
</profile>
```

Attribute	Values	Description
`device`	The device you want to configure in this <drive> section. You can use persistent device names via id, like `/dev/disk/by-id/ata-WDC_WD3200AAKS-75L9A0_WD-WMAV27368122` or *by-path*,like `/dev/disk/by-path/pci-0001:00:03.0-scsi-0:0:0:0`. `<device>/dev/sda</device>`	Optional. If left out, AutoYaST tries to guess the device. See *Tip: Skipping Devices* on how to influence guessing. A RAID must always have `/dev/md` as device.
`initialize`	If set to `true`, the partition table gets wiped out before AutoYaST starts the partition calculation. `<initialize config:type="boolean">true</initialize>`	Optional. The default is `false`.
`partitions`	A list of <partition> entries (see *Section 4.5.2, "Partition Configuration"*). `<partitions config:type="list"> <partition>...</partition>`	Optional. If no partitions are specified, AutoYaST will create a reasonable partitioning (see *Section 4.5.4, "Automated Partitioning"*).

Attribute	Values	Description
	`...` `</partitions>`	
`pesize`	This value only makes sense with LVM. `<pesize>8M</pesize>`	Optional. Default is 4M for LVM volume groups.
`use`	Specifies the strategy AutoYaST will use to partition the hard disk. Choose between: • `all` (uses the whole device while calculating the new partitioning), • `linux` (only existing Linux partitions are used), • `free` (only unused space on the device is used, no other partitions are touched), • 1,2,3 (a list of comma separated partition numbers to use).	This parameter should be provided.
`type`	Specify the type of the `drive`,	Optional. Default is `CT_DISK` for a normal physical hard disk.

Attribute	Values	Description
	Choose between: • `CT_DISK` for physical hard disks (default), • `CT_LVM` for LVM volume groups, `<type config:type="symbol">CT_LVM</type>`	
`disklabel`	Describes the type of the partition table. Choose between: • `msdos` • `gpt` `<disklabel>gpt</disklabel>`	Optional. By default YaST decides what makes sense.
`keep_unknown_lv`	This value only makes sense for type=CT_LVM drives. If you are reusing a logical volume group and you set this to `true`, all existing logical volumes in that group will not be touched unless they are specified in the <partitioning> section. So you can keep existing logical volumes without specifying them.	Optional. The default is `false`.

Attribute	Values	Description
	`<keep_unknown_lv config:type="boolean" >false</keep_unknown_lv>`	

Tip: Skipping Devices

You can influence AutoYaST's device-guessing for cases where you do not specify a <device> entry on your own. Usually AutoYaST would use the first device it can find that looks reasonable but you can configure it to skip some devices like this:

```
<partitioning config:type="list">
  <drive>
    <initialize config:type="boolean">true</initialize>
    <skip_list config:type="list">
      <listentry>
        <!-- skip devices that use the usb-storage driver -->
        <skip_key>driver</skip_key>
        <skip_value>usb-storage</skip_value>
      </listentry>
      <listentry>
        <!-- skip devices that are smaller than 1GB -->
        <skip_key>size_k</skip_key>
        <skip_value>1048576</skip_value>
        <skip_if_less_than config:type="boolean">true</skip_if_less_than>
      </listentry>
      <listentry>
        <!-- skip devices that are larger than 100GB -->
        <skip_key>size_k</skip_key>
        <skip_value>104857600</skip_value>
        <skip_if_more_than config:type="boolean">true</skip_if_more_than>
      </listentry>
    </skip_list>
  </drive>
</partitioning>
```

For a list of all possible <skip_key>, run **`yast2 ayast_probe`** on an already installed system.

4.5.2 Partition Configuration

The elements listed below must be placed within the following XML structure:

```
<drive>
  <partitions config:type="list">
    <partition>
      ...
    </partition>
  </partitions>
</drive>
```

Attribute	Values	Description
`create`	Specify if this partition must be created or if it already exists. `<create config:type="boolean" >false</create>`	If set to `false`, you also need to set `partition_nr` to tell AutoYaST the partition number.

`mount`	The mount point of this partition.
	`<mount>/</mount>`
	`<mount>swap</mount>`
		You should have at least a root partition (/) and a swap partition.

`fstopt`	Mount options for this partition.
	`<fstopt>`
	`ro,noatime,user,data=ordered,acl,user_xattr`
	`</fstopt>`
		See **`man mount`** for available mount options.

Attribute	Values	Description
`label`	The label of the partition (useful for the `mountby` parameter; see below). `<label>mydata</label>`	See **`man e2label`** for an example.
`uuid`	The uuid of the partition (only useful for the `mountby` parameter; see below). `<uuid >1b4e28ba-2fa1-11d2-883f-b9a761bde3fb</ uuid>`	See **`man uuidgen`**.
`size`	The size of the partition, for example 4G, 4500M, etc. The /boot partition and the swap partition can have `auto` as size. Then AutoYaST calculates a reasonable size. One partition can have the value `max` to use all remaining space. You can also specify the size in percentage. So 10% will use 10% of the size of the hard disk or volume group. You can mix auto, max, size, and percentage as you like. `<size>10G</size>`	
`format`	Specify if AutoYaST should format the partition. `<format config:type="boolean">false</ format>`	If you set `create` to `true`, then you likely want this option set to `true` as well.

Attribute	Values	Description
file system	Specify the file system to use on this partition: • btrfs • ext2 • ext3 • ext4 • fat • xfs • swap <filesystem config:type="symbol" >ext3</filesystem>	Optional. The default is btrfs for the root partition (/) and xfs for data partitions.
mkfs_options	Specify an option string that is added to the mkfs command. <mkfs_options>-I 128</mkfs_options>	Optional. Only use this when you know what you are doing.
partition_nr	The partition number of this partition. If you have set create=false or if you use LVM, then you can specify the partition via partition_nr. You can force AutoYaST to only create primary partitions by assigning numbers below 5. <partition_nr config:type="integer" >2</partition_nr>	Usually, numbers 1 to 4 are primary partitions while 5 and higher are logical partitions.

Attribute	Values	Description
`partition_id`	The `partition_id` sets the id of the partition. If you want different identifiers than 131 for Linux partition or 130 for swap, configure them with partition_id. `<partition_id config:type="integer">131</partition_id>`	The default is `131` for Linux partition and `130` for swap.
`mountby`	Instead of a partition number, you can tell AutoYaST to mount a partition by `device`, `label`, `uuid`, `path` or `id`, which are the udev path and udev id (see `/dev/disk/...`). `<mountby config:type="symbol">label</mountby>`	See `label` and `uuid` documentation above. The default depends on YaST and usually is `id`.

`subvolumes`	List of subvolumes to create for a file system of type Btrfs. This key only makes sense for file systems of type Btrfs. If there is a default subvolume used for the distribution (for example `@` in SUSE Linux Enterprise Server) the name of this default subvolume is automatically prepended to the names in this list.
	
	`<subvolumes config:type="list">`
	`  <path>tmp</path>`
	`  <path>opt</path>`
	`  <path>srv</path>`
	`  <path>var/crash</path>`
	`  <path>var/lock</path>`
	`  <path>var/run</path>`
	`  <path>var/tmp</path>`
	`  <path>var/spool</path>`	

Attribute	Values	Description
	... </subvolumes>	
lv_name	If this partition is in a logical volume in a volume group specify the logical volume name here (see the is_lvm_vg parameter in the drive configuration). <lv_name>opt_lv</lv_name>	
stripes	An integer that configures LVM striping. Specify across how many devices you want to stripe (spread data). <stripes config:type="integer">2</stripes>	
stripesize	Specify the size of each block in KB. <stripesize config:type="integer">4</stripesize>	
lvm_group	If this is a physical partition used by (part of) a volume group (LVM), you need to specify the name of the volume group here. <lvm_group>system</lvm_group>	
pool	pool must be set to true if the LVM logical volume should be an LVM thin pool. <pool config:type="boolean">false</pool>	

Attribute	Values	Description
`used_pool`	The name of the LVM thin pool that is used as a data store for this thin logical volume. If this is set to something non-empty, it implies that the volume is a so-called thin logical volume. `<used_pool>my_thin_pool</used_pool>`	
`raid_name`	If this physical volume is part of a RAID, specify the name of the RAID. `<raid_name>/dev/md0</raid_name>`	
`raid_type`	Specify the type of the RAID. `<raid_type>raid1</raid_type>`	
`raid_options`	Specify RAID options, see below. `<raid_options>...</raid_options>`	
`resize`	This boolean must be `true` if an existing partition should be resized. In this case, you want to set `create` to `false` and usually you do not want to `format` the partition. You need to tell AutoYaST the `partition_nr` and the `size`. The size can be in percentage of the original size or a number, like `800M`. `max` and `auto` do not work as size here. `<resize config:type="boolean" >false</resize>`	Resizing only works with physical disks, not with LVM volumes.

4.5.3 RAID Options

The following elements must be placed within the following XML structure:

```
<partition>
  <raid_options>
    ...
  </raid_options>
</partition>
```

Attribute	Values	Description
chunk_size	`<chunk_size>4</chunk_size>`	
parity_algorithm	Possible values are: left_asymmetric, left_symmetric, right_asymmetric, right_symmetric. For RAID6 and RAID10 the following values can be used: parity_first, parity_last, left_asymmetric_6, left_symmetric_6, right_asymmetric_6, right_symmetric_6, parity_first_6, n2, o2, f2, n3, o3, f3 for RAID6 and RAID10. `<parity_algorithm>left_asymmetric</parity_algorithm>`	

Attribute	Values	Description
raid_type	Possible values are: raid0, raid1 and raid5. `<raid_type>raid1</raid_type>`	The default is raid1.
device_order	This list contains the optional order of the physical devices: `<device_order config:type="list"> <device>/dev/sdb2</device> <device>/dev/sda1</device> ... </device_order>`	This is optional and the default is alphabetical order.

4.5.4 Automated Partitioning

For automated partitioning, you only need to provide the sizes and mount points of partitions. All other data needed for successful partitioning is calculated during installation—unless provided in the control file.

If no partitions are defined and the specified drive is also the drive where the root partition should be created, the following partitions are created automatically:

- /boot
  The size of the /boot partition is determined by the architecture of the target system.
- swap
  The size of the swap partition is determined by the amount of memory available in the system.
- / (root partition)

The size of the root partition is determined by the space left after creating swap and /boot.

Depending on the initial status of the drive and how it was previously partitioned, it is possible to create the default partitioning in the following ways:

Use Free Space
: If the drive is already partitioned, it is possible to create the new partitions using the free space on the hard disk. This requires the availability of sufficient space for all selected packages in addition to swap.

Reuse all available space
: Use this option to delete all existing partitions (Linux and non-Linux).

Reuse all available Linux partitions
: This option deletes all existing Linux partitions. Other partitions (for example Windows partitions) remain untouched. Note that this works only if the Linux partitions are at the end of the device.

Reuse only specified partitions
: This option allows you to select specific partitions to delete. Start the selection with the last available partition.

Repartitioning only works if the selected partitions are neighbors and located at the end of the device.

Important: Beware of Data Loss

The value provided in the use property determines how existing data and partitions are treated. The value all means that the entire disk will be erased. Make backups and use the confirm property if you need to keep some partitions with important data. Otherwise, no pop-ups will notify you about partitions being deleted.

If multiple drives are in the target system, identify all drives with their device names and specify how the partitioning should be performed.

Partition sizes can be given in gigabytes, megabytes or can be set to a flexible value using the keywords auto and max. max uses all available space on a drive, therefore should only be set for the last partition on the drive. With auto the size of a swap or boot partition is determined automatically, depending on the memory available and the type of the system.

A fixed size can be given as shown below:

`1GB`, `1G`, `100MB`, or `1000M` will all create a partition of the size 1 Gigabyte.

EXAMPLE 4.3: AUTOMATED PARTITIONING

The following is an example of a single drive system, which is not pre-partitioned and should be automatically partitioned according to the described pre-defined partition plan. If you do not specify the device, it will be automatically detected.

```
<partitioning  config:type="list">
  <drive>
    <device>/dev/sda</device>
    <use>all</use>
  </drive>
</partitioning>
```

A more detailed example shows how existing partitions and multiple drives are handled.

EXAMPLE 4.4: DETAILED AUTOMATED PARTITIONING

```
<partitioning  config:type="list">
  <drive>
    <device>/dev/sda</device>
    <partitions config:type="list">
      <partition>
 <mount>/</mount>
 <size>10G</size>
      </partition>
      <partition>
 <mount>swap</mount>
 <size>1G</size>
      </partition>
    </partitions>
  </drive>
  <drive>
    <device>/dev/sdb</device>
    <use>all</use>
```

```
    <partitions config:type="list">
      <partition>
  <filesystem  config:type="symbol">reiser</filesystem>
  <mount>/data1</mount>
  <size>15G</size>
      </partition>
      <partition>
  <filesystem  config:type="symbol">jfs</filesystem>
  <mount>/data2</mount>
  <size>auto</size>
      </partition>
    </partitions>
    <use>free</use>
  </drive>
</partitioning>
```

4.5.5 Advanced Partitioning Features

4.5.5.1 Wipe out Partition Table

Usually this is not needed because AutoYaST can delete partitions one by one automatically, but you need the option to let AutoYaST clear the partition table instead of deleting partitions individually.

Go to the `drive` section and add:

```
<initialize config:type="boolean">true</initialize>
```

With this setting AutoYaST will delete the partition table before it starts to analyze the actual partitioning and calculates its partition plan. Of course this means, that you cannot keep any of your existing partitions.

4.5.5.2 Mount Options

By default a file system to be mounted is identified in `/etc/fstab` by the device name. This identification can be changed so the file system is found by searching for a UUID or a volume label. Note that not all file systems can be mounted by UUID or a volume label. To specify how a partition is to be mounted, use the `mountby` property which has the `symbol` type. Possible options are:

- `device` (default)
- `label`
- `UUID`

If you choose to mount the partition using a label, the name entered for the `label` property is used as the volume label.

Add any valid mount option in the fourth field of `/etc/fstab`. Multiple options are separated by commas. Possible fstab options:

Mount read-only (`ro`)

No write access to the file system. Default is `false`.

No access time (`noatime`)

Access times are not updated when a file is read. Default is `false`.

Mountable by User (`user`)

The file system can be mounted by a normal user. Default is `false`.

Data Journaling Mode (`ordered`, `journal`, `writeback`)

`journal`

All data is committed to the journal prior to being written to the main file system.

`ordered`

All data is directly written to the main file system before its metadata is committed to the journal.

`writeback`

Data ordering is not preserved.

Access Control List (`acl`)

Enable access control lists on the file system.

Extended User Attributes (`user_xattr`)

Allow extended user attributes on the file system.

EXAMPLE 4.5: MOUNT OPTIONS

```
<partitions config:type="list">
  <partition>
    <filesystem config:type="symbol">reiser</filesystem>
    <format config:type="boolean">true</format>
    <fstopt>ro,noatime,user,data=ordered,acl,user_xattr</fstopt>
    <mount>/local</mount>
    <mountby config:type="symbol">uuid</mountby>
    <partition_id config:type="integer">131</partition_id>
    <size>10G</size>
  </partition>
</partitions>
```

4.5.5.3 Keeping Specific Partitions

In some cases you should leave partitions untouched and only format specific target partitions, rather than creating them from scratch. For example, if different Linux installations coexist, or you have another operating system installed, likely you do not want to wipe these out. You may also want to leave data partitions untouched.

Such scenarios require certain knowledge about the target systems and hard disks. Depending on the scenario, you might need to know the exact partition table of the target hard disk with partition ids, sizes and numbers. With this data you can tell AutoYaST to keep certain partitions, format others and create new partitions if needed.

The following example will keep partitions 1, 2 and 5 and delete partition 6 to create two new partitions. All remaining partitions will only be formatted.

EXAMPLE 4.6: KEEPING PARTITIONS

```
<partitioning config:type="list">
  <drive>
    <device>/dev/sdc</device>
      <partitions config:type="list">
        <partition>
```

```
        <create config:type="boolean">false</create>
        <format config:type="boolean">true</format>
        <mount>/</mount>
        <partition_nr config:type="integer">1</partition_nr>
      </partition>
      <partition>
        <create config:type="boolean">false</create>
        <format config:type="boolean">false</format>
        <partition_nr config:type="integer">2</partition_nr>
        <mount>/space</mount>
      </partition>
      <partition>
        <create config:type="boolean">false</create>
        <format config:type="boolean">true</format>
        <filesystem config:type="symbol">swap</filesystem>
        <partition_nr config:type="integer">5</partition_nr>
        <mount>swap</mount>
      </partition>
      <partition>
        <format config:type="boolean">true</format>
        <mount>/space2</mount>
        <size>5G</size>
      </partition>
      <partition>
        <format config:type="boolean">true</format>
        <mount>/space3</mount>
        <size>max</size>
      </partition>
    </partitions>
  <use>6</use>
 </drive>
</partitioning>
```

The last example requires exact knowledge of the existing partition table and the partition numbers of those partitions that should be kept. In some cases however, such data may not be available, especially in a mixed hardware environment with different hard disk types and configurations. The following scenario is for a system with a non-Linux OS with a designated area for a Linux installation.

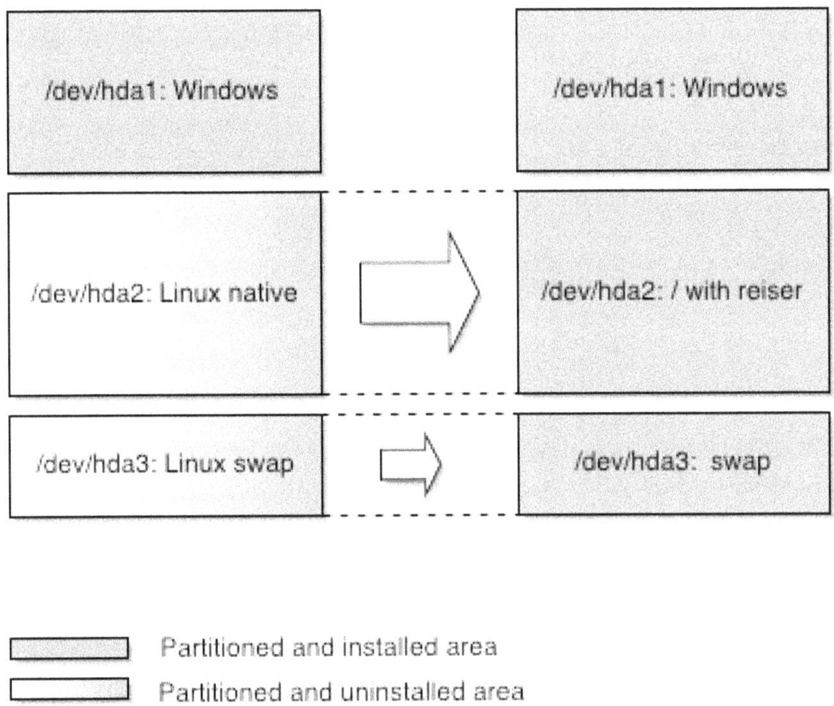

FIGURE 4.1: KEEPING PARTITIONS

In this scenario, shown in figure *Figure 4.1, "Keeping partitions"*, AutoYaST will not create new partitions. Instead it searches for certain partition types on the system and uses them according to the partitioning plan in the control file. No partition numbers are given in this case, only the mount points and the partition types (additional configuration data can be provided, for example file system options, encryption and file system type).

EXAMPLE 4.7: AUTO-DETECTION OF PARTITIONS TO BE KEPT.

```
<partitioning config:type="list">
  <drive>
    <partitions config:type="list">
      <partition>
        <create config:type="boolean">false</create>
```

```
        <format config:type="boolean">true</format>
        <mount>/</mount>
        <partition_id config:type="integer">131</partition_id>
      </partition>
      <partition>
        <create config:type="boolean">false</create>
        <format config:type="boolean">true</format>
        <filesystem config:type="symbol">swap</filesystem>
        <partition_id config:type="integer">130</partition_id>
        <mount>swap</mount>
      </partition>
    </partitions>
  </drive>
</partitioning>
```

4.5.6 Using an Existing Mount Table (fstab)

Note: This section does not work with the `partitioning` section together.

This section will be ignored if you have defined an own `partitioning` section too.

This option will allow AutoYaST to use an existing `/etc/fstab` and use the partition data from a previous installation. All partitions are kept and no new partitions are created. The partitions will be formatted and mounted as specified in `/etc/fstab` on a Linux root partition.

Although the default behavior is to format all partitions, it is also possible to leave some partitions untouched and only mount them, for example data partitions. If multiple installations are found on the system (multiple root partitions with different `fstab` files, the installation will abort, unless the root partition is configured in the control file. The following example illustrates how this option can be used:

EXAMPLE 4.8: READING AN EXISTING `/etc/fstab`

```
<partitioning_advanced>
  <fstab>
```

```
    <!-- Read data from existing fstab. If multiple root partitions are
            found, use the one specified below. Otherwise the first root
     partition is taken -->
    <!-- <root_partition>/dev/sda5</root_partition> -->
    <use_existing_fstab config:type="boolean">true</use_existing_fstab>
    <!-- all partitions found in fstab will be formatted and mounted
            by default unless a partition is listed below with different
     settings -->
    <partitions config:type="list">
      <partition>
        <format config:type="boolean">false</format>
        <mount>/bootmirror</mount>
      </partition>
    </partitions>
  </fstab>
</partitioning_advanced>
```

4.5.7 Logical Volume Manager (LVM)

To configure LVM, first create a physical volume using the normal partitioning method described above.

EXAMPLE 4.9: CREATE LVM PHYSICAL VOLUME

The following example shows how to prepare for LVM in the `partitioning` resource. A non-formatted partition is created on device `/dev/sda1` of the type `LVM` and with the volume group `system`. This partition will use all space available on the drive.

```
<partitioning config:type="list">
  <drive>
    <device>/dev/sda</device>
    <partitions config:type="list">
      <partition>
        <create config:type="boolean">true</create>
        <lvm_group>system</lvm_group>
        <partition_type>primary</partition_type>
        <partition_id config:type="integer">142</partition_id>
```

```
        <partition_nr config:type="integer">1</partition_nr>
        <size>max</size>
      </partition>
    </partitions>
    <use>all</use>
  </drive>
</partitioning>
```

EXAMPLE 4.10: LVM LOGICAL VOLUMES

```
<partitioning config:type="list">
  <drive>
    <device>/dev/sda</device>
    <partitions config:type="list">
      <partition>
        <lvm_group>system</lvm_group>
        <partition_type>primary</partition_type>
        <size>max</size>
      </partition>
    </partitions>
    <use>all</use>
  </drive>
  <drive>
    <device>/dev/system</device>
      <is_lvm_vg config:type="boolean">true</is_lvm_vg>
      <partitions config:type="list">
 <partition>
   <filesystem config:type="symbol">reiser</filesystem>
   <lv_name>user_lv</lv_name>
   <mount>/usr</mount>
   <size>15G</size>
 </partition>
 <partition>
   <filesystem config:type="symbol">reiser</filesystem>
   <lv_name>opt_lv</lv_name>
   <mount>/opt</mount>
   <size>10G</size>
```

```
  </partition>
  <partition>
    <filesystem config:type="symbol">reiser</filesystem>
    <lv_name>var_lv</lv_name>
    <mount>/var</mount>
    <size>1G</size>
  </partition>
       </partitions>
       <pesize>4M</pesize>
     <use>all</use>
   </drive>
</partitioning>
```

It is possible to set the `size` to `max` for the logical volumes. Of course, you can only use `max` for one(!) logical volume. You cannot set two logical volumes in one volume group to `max`.

4.5.8 Software RAID

Using AutoYaST, you can create and assemble software RAID devices. The supported RAID levels are the following:

RAID 0
: This level increases your disk performance. There is *no* redundancy in this mode. If one of the drives crashes, data recovery will not be possible.

RAID 1
: This mode offers the best redundancy. It can be used with two or more disks. An exact copy of all data is maintained on all disks. As long as at least one disk is still working, no data is lost. The partitions used for this type of RAID should have approximately the same size.

RAID 5
: This mode combines management of a larger number of disks and still maintains some redundancy. This mode can be used on three disks or more. If one disk fails, all data is still intact. If two disks fail simultaneously, all data is lost.

Multipath
: This mode allows access to the same physical device via multiple controllers for redundancy against a fault in a controller card. This mode can be used with at least two devices.

As with LVM, you need to create all RAID partitions first and assign them to the RAID device you want to create afterwards. Additionally you need to specify whether a partition or a device should be part of the RAID or if it should be a Spare device.

The following example shows a simple RAID1 configuration:

EXAMPLE 4.11: RAID1 CONFIGURATION

```
<partitioning config:type="list">
  <drive>
    <device>/dev/sda</device>
    <partitions config:type="list">
      <partition>
        <partition_id config:type="integer">253</partition_id>
        <format config:type="boolean">false</format>
        <raid_name>/dev/md0</raid_name>
        <raid_type>raid</raid_type>
        <size>4G</size>
      </partition>

 <!-- Insert a configuration for the regular partitions located on
         /dev/sda here (for example / and swap) -->

    </partitions>
    <use>all</use>
  </drive>
  <drive>
    <device>/dev/sdb</device>
    <partitions config:type="list">
      <partition>
        <format config:type="boolean">false</format>
        <partition_id config:type="integer">253</partition_id>
        <raid_name>/dev/md0</raid_name>
        <raid_type>raid</raid_type>
        <size>4gb</size>
      </partition>
    </partitions>
    <use>all</use>
```

```
  </drive>
  <drive>
    <device>/dev/md</device>
    <partitions config:type="list">
      <partition>
        <filesystem config:type="symbol">reiser</filesystem>
        <format config:type="boolean">true</format>
        <mount>/space</mount>
        <partition_id config:type="integer">131</partition_id>
        <partition_nr config:type="integer">0</partition_nr>
        <raid_options>
          <chunk_size>4</chunk_size>
          <parity_algorithm>left-asymmetric</parity_algorithm>
          <raid_type>raid1</raid_type>
        </raid_options>
      </partition>
    </partitions>
    <use>all</use>
  </drive>
</partitioning>
```

Keep the following in mind when configuring a RAID:

- The device for raid is always `/dev/md`
- The property `partition_nr` is used to determine the MD device number. If `partition_nr` is equal to 0, then `/dev/md0` is configured.
- All RAID-specific options are contained in the `raid_options` resource.

4.5.9 IBM System z Specific Configuration

4.5.9.1 Configuring DASD Disks

The elements listed below must be placed within the following XML structure:

```
<dasd>
```

```
 <devices config:type="list">
  <listentry>
   ...
  </listentry>
 </devices>
</dasd>
```

tags in the <profile> section. Each disk needs to be configured in a separate <listentry> ... </listentry> section.

Attribute	Values	Description
`device`	`DASD` is the only value allowed `<device >DASD</dev_name>`	
`dev_name`	The device (`dasdn`) you want to configure in this section. `<dev_name >/dev/dasda</dev_name>`	Optional but recommended. If left out, AutoYaST tries to guess the device.
`channel`	Channel by which the disk is accessed. `<channel>0.0.0150</ channel>`	Mandatory.
`diag`	Enable or disable the use of `DIAG`. Possible values are `true` (enable) or `false` (disable). `<diag`	Optional.

Attribute	Values	Description
	`config:type="boolean">true</diag>`	

4.5.9.2 Configuring zFCP Disks

The following elements must be placed within the following XML structure:

```
<profile>
  <zfcp>
    <devices config:type="list">
      <listentry>
        ...
      </listentry>
    </devices>
  </zfcp>
<profile>
```

Each disk needs to be configured in a separate `listentry` section.

Attribute	Values
`controller_id`	Channel number `<controller_id>0.0.fc00</controller_id>`

4.6 iSCSI Initiator Overview

Using the `iscsi-client` resource, you can configure the target machine as a iSCSI client.

EXAMPLE 4.12: ISCSI CLIENT

```
<iscsi-client>
```

```
  <initiatorname>iqn.2013-02.de.suse:01:e229358d2dea</initiatorname>
  <targets config:type="list">
    <listentry>
      <authmethod>None</authmethod>
      <portal>192.168.1.1:3260</portal>
      <startup>onboot</startup>
      <target>iqn.2001-05.com.doe:test</target>
      <iface>default</iface>
    </listentry>
  </targets>
  <version>1.0</version>
</iscsi-client>
```

Attribute	Description
initiatorname	`InitiatorName` is a value from `/etc/iscsi/initiatorname.iscsi`. In case you have iBFT, this value will be added from there and you are only able to change it in the BIOS setup.
version	Version of the YAST module. Default: 1.0
targets	List of targets. Each entry contains: `authmethod` Authentication method: None/CHAP `portal` Portal Address `startup` Value: manual/onboot `target` Target name `iface` Interface name

4.7 Country Settings

Language and timezone settings.

EXAMPLE 4.13: LANGUAGE

```
<language>
  <language>en_GB</language>
  <languages>de_DE,en_GB</languages>
</language>
```

A list of available languages can be found under /usr/share/YaST2/data/languages

Attribute	Description
language	Primary language.
language	Secondary languages seperated by commas

EXAMPLE 4.14: TIMEZONE

```
<timezone>
  <hwclock>UTC</hwclock>
  <timezone>Europe/Berlin</timezone>
</timezone>
```

Attribute	Values
hwclock	localtime/UTC
timezone	A list of available timezones can be found under /usr/share/YaST2/data/timezone_raw.ycp

4.8 Software

4.8.1 Package Selection with Patterns

Patterns are configured like this:

EXAMPLE 4.15: PACKAGE SELECTION IN THE CONTROL FILE WITH PATTERNS

```
<software>
  <patterns config:type="list">
    <pattern>directory_server</pattern>
  </patterns>
  <packages  config:type="list">
    <package>apache</package>
    <package>postfix</package>
  </packages>
  <do_online_update config:type="boolean">true</do_online_update>
</software>
```

4.8.2 Installing Additional and Customized Packages

In addition to the packages available for installation on the DVD-ROMs, you can add external packages including customized kernels. Customized kernel packages must be compatible to the SUSE packages and must install the kernel files to the same locations.

Unlike in earlier in versions, you do not need a special resource in the control file to install custom and external packages. Instead you need to re-create the package database and update it with any new packages or new package versions in the source repository.

A script is provided for this task which will query packages available in the repository and create the package database. Use the command **`/usr/bin/create_package_descr`**. When creating the database, all languages will be reset to English.

EXAMPLE 4.16: CREATING PACKAGE DATABASE

```
cd /usr/local/DVDs/LATEST/suse
create_package_descr -x PATH_TO_EXTRA_PROV -d /usr/local/CDs/LATEST/suse
```

In the above example, the directory `/usr/local/CDs/LATEST/suse` contains the architecture dependent (for example `x86_64`) and architecture independent packages (`noarch`). This might look different on other architectures.

The advantage of this method is that you can keep an up-to-date repository with fixed and updated package. Additionally this method makes the creation of custom CD-ROMs easier.

To add your own RPMs to an installation source (or a module such as the SDK), add a file `add_on_products` to the installation source.

```
media_url [path_on_media [product_1 [product_2 [....]]]
```

`media_url` is the URL of the media, `path_on_media` is the path to the catalog on the media. If not present, / (root) is assumed. `product_1` and following are the names of products, which should be marked for installation. If no product is specified, all products found on the media are selected for installation. For example:

```
http://192.168.66.6/SLES/sdk/DVD1
        http://192.168.66.6/SLES/DVD1/updates
```

As an alternative to adding the `add_on_products` file to the installation source, you can use the AutoYaST control file to specify modules, extensions and add-on products. For example:

```
<add-on>
  <add_on_products config:type="list">
    <listentry>
      <media_url>http://192.168.66.6/SLES/DVD1/updates</media_url>
      <product>SLES_Updates</product>
      <alias>SuSE-Updates</alias>
      <product_dir>/</product_dir>
      <priority config:type="integer">20</priority>
      <ask_on_error config:type="boolean">false</ask_on_error>
      <name>MyUpdates</name> <
    </listentry>
  </add_on_products>
</add-on>
```

AutoYaST can ask the user to make add-on products, modules or extension available instead of reporting a time-out error when no repository can be found at the given location. Set ask_on_error to `true` (the default is `false`).

If you want to use unsigned installation sources with AutoYaST, turn off the checks with the following configuration in your AutoYaST control file.

The elements listed below must be placed within the following XML structure:

```
<general>
  <signature-handling>
    ...
  </signature-handling>
</general>
```

Default values for all options are `false`. If an option is set to `false` and a package or repository fails the respective test, it is silently ignored and will not be installed. Note that setting any of these options to `true` is a potential security risk. Never do it when using packages or repositories from third party sources.

Attribute	Values
`accept_unsigned_file`	If set to `true`, AutoYaST will accept unsigned files like the content file. `<accept_unsigned_file config:type="boolean" >true</accept_unsigned_file>`
`accept_file_without_checksum`	If set to `true`, AutoYaST will accept files without a checksum in the content file. `<accept_file_without_checksum config:type="boolean" >true</accept_file_without_checksum>`
`accept_verification_failed`	If set to `true`, AutoYaST will accept signed files even when the verification of the signature failed. `<accept_verification_failed config:type="boolean" >true</accept_verification_failed>`

Attribute	Values
`accept_unknown_gpg_key`	If set to `true`, AutoYaST will accept new gpg keys on the installation source, for example the key used to sign the content file. `<accept_unknown_gpg_key config:type="boolean" >true</accept_unknown_gpg_key>`
`accept_non_trusted_gpg_key`	This means, the key is known, but is not trusted by you. `<accept_non_trusted_gpg_key config:type="boolean" >true</accept_non_trusted_gpg_key>`
`import_gpg_key`	If set to `true`, AutoYaST will accept and import new gpg keys on the installation source in its database. `<import_gpg_key config:type="boolean" >true</import_gpg_key>`

It is possible to configure the signature handling for each add-on product, module, or extension individually. The following elements must be between the `signature-handling` section of the individual add-on product, module, or extension. All settings are optional. If not configured, the global signature-handling from the `general` section is used.

Attribute	Values
`accept_unsigned_file`	If set to `true`, AutoYaST will accept unsigned files like the content file for this add-on product. `<accept_unsigned_file config:type="boolean"`

Attribute	Values
	>true</accept_unsigned_file>
accept_file_without_checksum	If set to true, AutoYaST will accept files without a checksum in the content file for this add-on. <accept_file_without_checksum config:type="boolean" >true</accept_file_without_checksum>
accept_verification_failed	If set to true, AutoYaST will accept signed files even when the verification of the signature fails. <accept_verification_failed config:type="boolean" >true</accept_verification_failed>
accept_unknown_gpg_key	If set to true, AutoYaST will accept new gpg keys on the installation source, for example the key used to sign the content file. <accept_unknown_gpg_key> <all config:type="boolean">false</ all> <keys config:type="list"> <keyid>3B3011B76B9D6523</keyid> </keys> </accept_unknown_gpg_key>
accept_non_trusted_gpg_key	This means, the key is known, but it is not trusted by you. <accept_non_trusted_gpg_key>

Attribute	Values

	`<all config:type="boolean">false</all>`
	`<keys config:type="list">`
	`<keyid>3B3011B76B9D6523</keyid>`
	`</keys>`
	`</accept_non_trusted_gpg_key>`

`import_gpg_key`	If set to `true`, AutoYaST will accept and import new gpg keys on the installation source into its database.
	`<import_gpg_key>`
	`<all config:type="boolean">false</all>`
	`<keys config:type="list">`
	`<keyid>3B3011B76B9D6523</keyid>`
	`</keys>`
	`</import_gpg_key>`

4.8.3 Kernel Packages

Kernel packages are not part of any selection. The required kernel is determined during installation. If the kernel package is added to any selection or to the individual package selection, installation will mostly fail because of conflicts.

To force the installation of a specific kernel, use the `kernel` property. The following is an example of forcing the installation of the default kernel. This kernel will be installed even if an SMP or other kernel is required.

EXAMPLE 4.17: KERNEL SELECTION IN THE CONTROL FILE

```
<software>
  <kernel>kernel-default</kernel>
  ...
</software>
```

4.8.4 Removing Automatically Selected Packages

Some packages are selected automatically either because of a dependency or because it is available in a selection.

Removing such packages might break the system consistency and it is not recommended to remove basic packages unless a replacement which provides the same services is provided. The best example for this case are mail transfer agent (MTA) packages. By default, `postfix` will be selected and installed. If you want to use another MTA like `sendmail`, then postfix can be removed from the list of selected package using a list in the software resource. However, note that sendmail is not shipped with SUSE Linux Enterprise Server. The following example shows how this can be done:

EXAMPLE 4.18: PACKAGE SELECTION IN CONTROL FILE

```
<software>
  <packages  config:type="list">
    <package>sendmail</package>
  </packages>
  <remove-packages  config:type="list">
    <package>postfix</package>
  </remove-packages>
</software>
```

Note: Package Removal Failure

Note that it is not possible to remove a package, that is part of a pattern (see *Section 4.8.1, "Package Selection with Patterns"*). When specifying such a package for removal, the installation will fail with the following error message:

```
The package resolver run failed. Please check
      your software section in the autoyast profile.
```

4.8.5 Installing Packages in Stage 2

If you want to install packages after the reboot during stage two, instead of during the normal installation process in stage one, you can use the `post-packages` element for that:

```
<software>
  <post-packages config:type="list">
    <package>yast2-cim</package>
  </post-packages>
</software>
```

4.8.6 Installing Patterns in Stage 2

You can also install patterns in stage 2. Use the `post-patterns` element for that:

```
<software>
  <post-patterns config:type="list">
    <pattern>apparmor</pattern>
  </post-patterns>
</software>
```

4.8.7 Online Update in Stage 2

You can perform an online update at the end of the installation. Set the boolean `do_online_update` to `true`. Of course this only makes sense if you add an online update repository in the suse-register/customer-center section, for example, or in a post-script. If the online update repository was already available in stage one via the add-on section, then AutoYaST has already installed the latest packages available. If a kernel update is done via online-update, a reboot at the end of stage two is triggered.

```
<software>
  <do_online_update config:type="boolean">true</do_online_update>
</software>
```

4.9 SUSE registration

AutoYaST also supports the registration of a SUSE Linux Enterprise (SLE) product to the SUSE Customer Center or SMT (Subscription Management Tool). The module is a part of SLE product installation or upgrade workflow. So it is not needed for Tumbleweed or Leap. A registered system will receive security updates and the functionality of the system can be extented via online extensions or modules.

4.9.1 Registration section

EXAMPLE 4.19: SUSE REGISTRATION

```
<suse_register>
      <do_registration config:type="boolean">true</do_registration>
      <install_updates config:type="boolean">true</install_updates>
      <email>user@example.com</email>
      <reg_code>your_reg_code</reg_code>
      </reg_server>
      </reg_server_cert>
      <slp_discovery config:type="boolean">false</slp_discovery>
      <addons config:type="list">
       <addon>
        <name>sle-sdk</name>
        <version>12</version>
        <arch>x86_64</arch>
        <release_type>nil</release_type>
       </addon>
      </addons>
     </suse_register>
```

Element	Description	Comment
do_registration	If set to `false` all other options are ignored and the system is not registered.	

Element	Description	Comment
reg_server	If you use SMT specify the server URL here.	Optional. Default `scc.suse.com`
reg_server_cert	Download the server SSL certificate from the specified URL.	Optional. Not recommended
reg_server_cert_fingerprint_type	Server SSL certificate fingerprint - the matching certificate will be automatically imported when the SSL communication fails because of verification error, the type can be either `SHA1` or `SHA256`, write the appropriate checksum value into the `reg_server_cert_fingerprint` tag (this is more secure than using the `reg_server_cert` tag which does not check the authenticity of the downloaded SSL certificate at all)	Optional
reg_server_cert_fingerprint	Fingerprint value, use hexadecimal notation, separate the pairs by double colon (:), comparison is case insensitive (i.e. you can use both [a-f] and [A-F] characters in hexadecimal numbers)	Optional
email	Email matching the registration code.	Required

Element	Description	Comment
reg_code	Registration code, might be empty when a SMT server is used.	Required for `scc.suse.com` registration.
install_updates	Whether to install the updates from the Update channels.	
slp_discovery	Obtain the registration server URL from SLP discovery, exactly one server is expected to be found, if there are more servers found Yast cannot automatically choose one of them and the installation fails (in that case use `reg_server` tag and hardcode the required registration server URL).	
addons	Register additional extensions or modules	Described in the next section

4.9.2 Available SCC Extensions

Here are listed currently available extensions for SLES-12-x86_64 which can be used in Autoyast profile.

Note: The list is product and architecture dependent, e.g. only the `sle-sdk` extension is available for SLED and some SLES extensions are not available for all architectures.

Extensions `sle-we`, `sle-ha` and `sle-ha-geo` require a registration code.

EXAMPLE 4.20: SCC EXTENTIONS

```
<addons config:type="list">
 <addon>
```

```
      <arch>x86_64</arch>
      <name>sle-ha</name>
      <reg_code>YOUR_REG_CODE_HERE</reg_code>
      <release_type>nil</release_type>
      <version>12</version>
    </addon>
    <addon>
      <arch>x86_64</arch>
      <name>sle-ha-geo</name>
      <reg_code>YOUR_REG_CODE_HERE</reg_code>
      <release_type>nil</release_type>
      <version>12</version>
    </addon>
    <addon>
      <arch>x86_64</arch>
      <name>sle-module-web-scripting</name>
      <reg_code/>
      <release_type>nil</release_type>
      <version>12</version>
    </addon>
    <addon>
      <arch>x86_64</arch>
      <name>sle-module-adv-systems-management</name>
      <reg_code/>
      <release_type>nil</release_type>
      <version>12</version>
    </addon>
    <addon>
      <arch>x86_64</arch>
      <name>sle-module-legacy</name>
      <reg_code/>
      <release_type>nil</release_type>
      <version>12</version>
    </addon>
    <addon>
      <arch>x86_64</arch>
```

```
      <name>sle-we</name>
      <reg_code>YOUR_REG_CODE_HERE</reg_code>
      <release_type>nil</release_type>
      <version>12</version>
    </addon>
    <addon>
      <arch>x86_64</arch>
      <name>sle-sdk</name>
      <reg_code/>
      <release_type>nil</release_type>
      <version>12</version>
    </addon>
    <addon>
      <arch>x86_64</arch>
      <name>sle-module-public-cloud</name>
      <reg_code/>
      <release_type>nil</release_type>
      <version>12</version>
    </addon>
```

4.10 Upgrade

AutoYaST can also be used for doing a system upgrade. Besides upgrading packages, following sections are supported too:

- `scripts/pre-scripts` Running user scripts very early, before anything else really happens.
- `add-on` Defining an additional add-on product.
- `language` Setting the used language.
- `timezone` Setting timezone.
- `keyboard` Setting keyboard.

- `software` Installing additional software/patterns. Removing installed packages.
- `suse_register` Running registration process.

In order to control the upgrade process following sections can be defined:

EXAMPLE 4.21: UPGRADE AND BACKUP

```
<upgrade>
    <only_installed_packages config:type="boolean">true</only_installed_packages>
    <stop_on_solver_conflict config:type="boolean">true</stop_on_solver_conflict>
  </upgrade>
  <backup>
    <sysconfig config:type="boolean">true</sysconfig>
    <modified config:type="boolean">true</modified>
    <remove_old config:type="boolean">true</remove_old>
  </backup>
```

Element	Description	Comment
only_installed_packages	Update only installed packages and do not add additional one due e.g. recommendations.	
stop_on_solver_conflict	Halt installation if there are package dependencies issues.	
modified	Create backup of modified files.	
sysconfig	Create backup of `/etc/sysconfig` directory.	
remove_old	Remove backups from previous updates.	

Note: Starting AutoYaST in upgrade mode

In order to start the AutoYaST upgrade mode you have to use following linuxrc parameters:

`autoupgrade=1 autoyast=http://..,`

4.11 Services and Targets

With the `services-manager` resource you can set the default systemd target and specify in detail which system services you want to start or deactivate.

The `default-target` property specifies the default systemd target into which the system boots. Valid options are `graphical` for a graphical login, or `multi-user` for a console login.

The <enable config:type="list"> and <disable config:type="list"> let you explicitly enable or disable services.

EXAMPLE 4.22: CONFIGURING SERVICES AND TARGETS

```
<services-manager>
  <default_target>multi-user</default_target>
  <services>
    <disable config:type="list">
      <service>cups</service>
    </disable>
    <enable config:type="list">
      <service>sshd</service>
    </enable>
  </services>
</services-manager>
```

4.12 Network Configuration

Network configuration is used to connect a single workstation to an Ethernet-based LAN or to configure a dial-up connection. More complex configurations (multiple network cards, routing, etc.) are also provided.

If the following setting is set to `true` YaST will keep network settings created during the installation (via Linuxrc) and/or merge it with network settings from the AutoYaST control file (if defined). AutoYaST settings have higher priority than already present configuration files. YaST will write ifcfg-* files based on the entries in the control file without removing old ones. If there is an empty or no dns and routing section, YaST will keep already existing values. Otherwise settings from the control file will be applied.

```
<keep_install_network
config:type="boolean">true</keep_install_network>
```

To configure network settings and activate networking automatically, one global resource is used to store the whole network configuration.

EXAMPLE 4.23: NETWORK CONFIGURATION

```
<networking>
  <dns>
    <dhcp_hostname config:type="boolean">true</dhcp_hostname>
    <domain>site</domain>
    <hostname>linux-bqua</hostname>
    <nameservers config:type="list">
      <nameserver>192.168.1.116</nameserver>
      <nameserver>192.168.1.117</nameserver>
      <nameserver>192.168.1.118</nameserver>
    </nameservers>
    <resolv_conf_policy>auto</resolv_conf_policy>
    <searchlist config:type="list">
      <search>example.com</search>
      <search>example.net</search>
    </searchlist>
    <write_hostname config:type="boolean">false</write_hostname>
  </dns>
  <interfaces config:type="list">
    <interface>
      <bootproto>dhcp</bootproto>
      <device>eth0</device>
      <startmode>auto</startmode>
```

```
    </interface>
    <interface>
      <bootproto>static</bootproto>
      <broadcast>127.255.255.255</broadcast>
      <device>lo</device>
      <firewall>no</firewall>
      <ipaddr>127.0.0.1</ipaddr>
      <netmask>255.0.0.0</netmask>
      <network>127.0.0.0</network>
      <prefixlen>8</prefixlen>
      <startmode>nfsroot</startmode>
      <usercontrol>no</usercontrol>
    </interface>
  </interfaces>
  <ipv6 config:type="boolean">true</ipv6>
  <keep_install_network config:type="boolean">false</keep_install_network>
  <managed config:type="boolean">false</managed>        ###### NetworkManager ?
  <net-udev config:type="list">
    <rule>
      <name>eth0</name>
      <rule>ATTR{address}</rule>
      <value>00:30:6E:08:EC:80</value>
    </rule>
  </net-udev>
  <s390-devices config:type="list">
    <listentry>
      <chanids>0.0.0800 0.0.0801 0.0.0802</chanids>
      <type>qeth</type>
    </listentry>
  </s390-devices>
  <routing>
    <ipv4_forward config:type="boolean">false</ipv4_forward>
    <ipv6_forward config:type="boolean">false</ipv6_forward>
    <routes config:type="list">
      <route>
        <destination>192.168.2.1</destination>
```

```
        <device>eth0</device>
        <extrapara>foo</extrapara>
        <gateway>-</gateway>
        <netmask>-</netmask>
      </route>
      <route>
        <destination>default</destination>
        <device>eth0</device>
        <gateway>192.168.1.1</gateway>
        <netmask>-</netmask>
      </route>
      <route>
        <destination>default</destination>
        <device>lo</device>
        <gateway>192.168.5.1</gateway>
        <netmask>-</netmask>
      </route>
    </routes>
  </routing>
</networking>
```

Tip: IPv6 Address Support

Using IPv6 addresses in AutoYaST is fully supported. To disable IPv6 Address Support, set <ipv6 config:type="boolean">false</ipv6>

4.12.1 Persistent Names of Network Interfaces

The following elements must be between the <net-udev>...</net-udev> tags.

Element	Description	Comment
name	Network interface name, e.g. `eth3`	required

Element	Description	Comment
rule	`ATTR{address}` for a MAC based rule, `KERNELS` for a bus ID based rule	required
value	e.g. `f0:de:f1:6b:da:69` for a MAC rule, `0000:00:1c.1 or 0.0.0700` for a bus ID rule	required

4.12.2 s390 Devices

The following elements must be between the <s390-devices>...</s390-devices> tags.

Element	Description	Comment
type	qeth, ctc or iucv	
chanids	channel ids separated by spaces `<chanids>0.0.0700 0.0.0701 0.0.0702</chanids>`	
layer2	`<layer2 config:type="boolean">true</layer2>`	boolean; default: false
portname	QETH port name	
protocol	CTC / LCS protocol, a small number (as a string) `<protocol>1</protocol>`	optional

Element	Description	Comment
router	IUCV router/user	

4.12.3 Proxy

Configure your Internet proxy (caching) settings.

Configure proxies for HTTP and FTP with `http_proxy` and `ftp_proxy`, respectively. Addresses or names that should be directly accessible need to be specified with `no_proxy` (space separated values). If you are using a proxy server with authorization, fill in `proxy_user` and `proxy_password`,

EXAMPLE 4.24: NETWORK CONFIGURATION: PROXY

```
<proxy>
  <enabled config:type="boolean">true</enabled>
  <ftp_proxy>http://192.168.1.240:3128</ftp_proxy>
  <http_proxy>http://192.168.1.240:3128</http_proxy>
  <no_proxy>localhost</no_proxy>
  <proxy_password>testpw</proxy_password>
  <proxy_user>testuser</proxy_user>
</proxy>
```

4.12.4 (X)Inetd

The control file has elements to specify which superserver should be used (netd_service), whether it should be enabled (netd_status) and how the services should be configured (netd_conf).

A service description element has two parts: key and non-key. When writing the configuration, services are matched using the key fields; to the matching service, non-key fields are applied. If no service matches, it is created. If more services match, a warning is reported. The key fields are *script, service, protocol and server.*

service and *protocol* are matched literally. *script* is the base name of the configuration file: usually a file in `/etc/xinetd.d`, for example "echo-udp", or "inetd.conf". For compatibility with 8.2, *server* is matched more loosely: if it is `/usr/sbin/tcpd`, the real server name is taken from *server_args*. After that, the basename of the first whitespace-separated word is taken and these values are compared.

Note

Since SUSE Linux Enterprise Server 12 SP1 it is possible to configure the network for the installed system while the first installation stage. In that case you have to set

```
<second_stage config:type="boolean">false</second_stage>
```

in the `general/mode` section.

EXAMPLE 4.25: INETD EXAMPLE

```
<profile>
  <inetd>
    <netd_service config:type="symbol">xinetd</netd_service>
    <netd_status config:type="integer">0</netd_status>
    <netd_conf config:type="list">
      <conf>
 <script>imap</script>
 <service>pop3</service>
 <enabled config:type="boolean">true</enabled>
      </conf>
      <conf>
 <server>in.ftpd</server>
 <server_args>-A</server_args>
 <enabled config:type="boolean">true</enabled>
      </conf>
      <conf>
 <service>daytime</service>
 <protocol>tcp</protocol>
      </conf>
      <conf>...</conf>
```

```
    </netd_conf>
  </inetd>
</profile>
```

4.13 NIS Client

Using the `nis` resource, you can configure the target machine as a NIS client. The following example shows a detailed configuration using multiple domains.

EXAMPLE 4.26: NETWORK CONFIGURATION: NIS

```
<nis>
  <nis_broadcast config:type="boolean">true</nis_broadcast>
  <nis_broken_server config:type="boolean">true</nis_broken_server>
  <nis_by_dhcp config:type="boolean">false</nis_by_dhcp>
  <nis_domain>test.com</nis_domain>
  <nis_local_only config:type="boolean">true</nis_local_only>
  <nis_options></nis_options>
  <nis_other_domains config:type="list">
    <nis_other_domain>
      <nis_broadcast config:type="boolean">false</nis_broadcast>
      <nis_domain>domain.com</nis_domain>
      <nis_servers config:type="list">
        <nis_server>10.10.0.1</nis_server>
      </nis_servers>
    </nis_other_domain>
  </nis_other_domains>
  <nis_servers config:type="list">
    <nis_server>192.168.1.1</nis_server>
  </nis_servers>
  <start_autofs config:type="boolean">true</start_autofs>
  <start_nis config:type="boolean">true</start_nis>
</nis>
```

4.14 NIS Server

You can configure the target machine as a NIS server. NIS Master Server and NIS Slave Server and a combination of both is available.

EXAMPLE 4.27: NIS SERVER CONFIGURATION

```
<nis_server>
  <domain>mydomain.de</domain>
  <maps_to_serve config:type="list">
    <nis_map>auto.master</nis_map>
    <nis_map>ethers</nis_map>
  </maps_to_serve>
  <merge_passwd config:type="boolean">false</merge_passwd>
  <mingid config:type="integer">0</mingid>
  <minuid config:type="integer">0</minuid>
  <nopush config:type="boolean">false</nopush>
  <pwd_chfn config:type="boolean">false</pwd_chfn>
  <pwd_chsh config:type="boolean">false</pwd_chsh>
  <pwd_srcdir>/etc</pwd_srcdir>
  <securenets config:type="list">
    <securenet>
      <netmask>255.0.0.0</netmask>
      <network>127.0.0.0</network>
    </securenet>
  </securenets>
  <server_type>master</server_type>
  <slaves config:type="list"/>
  <start_ypbind config:type="boolean">false</start_ypbind>
  <start_yppasswdd config:type="boolean">false</start_yppasswdd>
  <start_ypxfrd config:type="boolean">false</start_ypxfrd>
</nis_server>
```

Attribute	Values	Description
`domain`	NIS domain name	

Attribute	Values	Description
maps_to_serve	List of maps which are available for the server.	Values: auto.master, ethers, group, hosts, netgrp, networks, passwd, protocols, rpc, services, shadow
merge_passwd	Select if your passwd file should be merged with the shadow file (only possible if the shadow file exists).	Value: true/false
mingid	Minimal GID to include in the user maps.	
minuid	Minimal UID to include in the user maps.	
nopush	Don't push the changes to slave servers. (useful if there aren't any)	Value: true/false
pwd_chfn	YPPWD_CHFN - allow changing the full name?	Value: true/false
pwd_chsh	YPPWD_CHSH - allow changing the login shell?	Value: true/false
pwd_srcdir	YPPWD_SRCDIR - source directory for passwd data	Default: /etc
securenets	List of allowed hosts to query the NIS server	A host address will be allowed if network is equal to the bitwise AND of the host's address and the netmask.

Attribute	Values	Description
		The entry with netmask 255.0.0.0 and network 127.0.0.0 must exist to allow connections from the local host. Entering netmask 0.0.0.0 and network 0.0.0.0 gives access to all hosts.
`server_type`	Select whether to configure the NIS server as a master or a slave or not to configure a NIS server.	Values: master, slave, none
`slaves`	List of hostnames to configure as NIS server slaves.	
`start_ypbind`	This host is also a NIS client (only when client is configured locally).	Value: true/false
`start_ypbind`	This host is also a NIS client (only when client is configured locally).	Value: true/false
`start_yppasswdd`	Start also the password daemon?	Value: true/false
`start_ypxfrd`	Start also the map transfer daemon. Fast Map distribution - it will speed up the transfer of maps to the slaves.	Value: true/false

4.15 LDAP Server (Authentication Server)

Using the `auth-server` resource, you can configure the target machine as a LDAP server. The following example shows a detailed configuration.

EXAMPLE 4.28: LDAP CONFIGURATION

```
<auth-server>
  <daemon>
    <listeners config:type="list">
      <listentry>ldap</listentry>
      <listentry>ldapi</listentry>
    </listeners>
    <serviceEnabled>1</serviceEnabled>
    <slp/>
  </daemon>
  <databases config:type="list">
    <listentry>
      <access config:type="list">
        <listentry>
          <access config:type="list">
            <listentry>
              <control/>
              <level>write</level>
              <type>self</type>
              <value/>
            </listentry>
            <listentry>
              <control/>
              <level>auth</level>
              <type>*</type>
              <value/>
            </listentry>
          </access>
          <target>
            <attrs>userPassword</attrs>
          </target>
```

```
        </listentry>
        <listentry>
          <access config:type="list">
            <listentry>
              <control/>
              <level>write</level>
              <type>self</type>
              <value/>
            </listentry>
            <listentry>
              <control/>
              <level>read</level>
              <type>*</type>
              <value/>
            </listentry>
          </access>
          <target>
            <attrs>shadowLastChange</attrs>
          </target>
        </listentry>
        <listentry>
          <access config:type="list">
            <listentry>
              <control/>
              <level>read</level>
              <type>self</type>
              <value/>
            </listentry>
            <listentry>
              <control/>
              <level>none</level>
              <type>*</type>
              <value/>
            </listentry>
          </access>
          <target>
```

```
        <attrs>userPKCS12</attrs>
      </target>
    </listentry>
    <listentry>
      <access config:type="list">
        <listentry>
          <control/>
          <level>read</level>
          <type>*</type>
          <value/>
        </listentry>
      </access>
      <target/>
    </listentry>
  </access>
  <checkpoint config:type="list">
    <listentry>1024</listentry>
    <listentry>5</listentry>
  </checkpoint>
  <directory>/var/lib/ldap</directory>
  <entrycache>10000</entrycache>
  <idlcache>30000</idlcache>
  <indexes>
    <cn>
      <eq>1</eq>
      <sub>1</sub>
    </cn>
    <displayName>
      <eq>1</eq>
      <sub>1</sub>
    </displayName>
    <gidNumber>
      <eq>1</eq>
    </gidNumber>
    <givenName>
      <eq>1</eq>
```

```
          <sub>1</sub>
        </givenName>
        <mail>
          <eq>1</eq>
        </mail>
        <member>
          <eq>1</eq>
        </member>
        <memberUid>
          <eq>1</eq>
        </memberUid>
        <objectclass>
          <eq>1</eq>
        </objectclass>
        <sn>
          <eq>1</eq>
          <sub>1</sub>
        </sn>
        <uid>
          <eq>1</eq>
          <sub>1</sub>
        </uid>
        <uidNumber>
          <eq>1</eq>
        </uidNumber>
      </indexes>
      <rootdn>cn=Administrator,DC=corp,DC=Fabrikam,DC=COM,CN=Karen Berge</rootdn>
      <rootpw>{SSHA}LCdgE3gNejqBogGI3aclXf4DOIVMSk9ZQg==</rootpw>
      <suffix>DC=corp,DC=Fabrikam,DC=COM,CN=Karen Berge</suffix>
      <type>hdb</type>
    </listentry>
  </databases>
  <globals>
    <allow config:type="list"/>
    <disallow config:type="list"/>
    <loglevel config:type="list">
```

```
      <listentry>none</listentry>
    </loglevel>
    <tlsconfig>
      <caCertDir/>
      <caCertFile/>
      <certFile/>
      <certKeyFile/>
      <crlCheck>0</crlCheck>
      <crlFile/>
      <verifyClient>0</verifyClient>
    </tlsconfig>
  </globals>
  <schema config:type="list">
    <listentry>
      <definition>dn: cn=schema,cn=config
          objectClass: olcSchemaConfig
          ......
          .....
          ....
          ...
          ..
          .
      </definition>
      <name>schema</name>
    </listentry>
    <listentry>
      <includeldif>/etc/openldap/schema/core.ldif</includeldif>
    </listentry>
    <listentry>
      <includeldif>/etc/openldap/schema/cosine.ldif</includeldif>
    </listentry>
    <listentry>
      <includeldif>/etc/openldap/schema/inetorgperson.ldif</includeldif>
    </listentry>
    <listentry>
      <includeschema>/etc/openldap/schema/rfc2307bis.schema</includeschema>
```

```
      </listentry>
      <listentry>
        <includeschema>/etc/openldap/schema/yast.schema</includeschema>
      </listentry>
    </schema>
  </auth-server>
```

4.16 Windows Domain Membership

Using the samba-client resource, you can configure a membership of a workgroup, NT domain, or Active Directory domain.

EXAMPLE 4.29: SAMBA CLIENT CONFIGURATION

```
<samba-client>
  <disable_dhcp_hostname config:type="boolean">true</disable_dhcp_hostname>
  <global>
    <security>domain</security>
    <usershare_allow_guests>No</usershare_allow_guests>
    <usershare_max_shares>100</usershare_max_shares>
    <workgroup>WORKGROUP</workgroup>
  </global>
  <winbind config:type="boolean">false</winbind>
</samba-client>
```

Attribute	Values	Description
disable_dhcp_hostname	Do not allow DHCP to change the hostname.	Value: true/false
disable_dhcp_hostname	Do not allow DHCP to change the hostname.	Value: true/false

Attribute	Values	Description
global/security	Kind of authentication regime (domain technology or Active Directory server (ADS))	Value: ADS/domain
global/usershare_allow_guests	Shares guest access is allowed.	Value: No/Yes
global/usershare_max_shares	Number of max shares from smb.conf	0 means that shares are not enabled.
global/workgroup	Workgroup or domain name.	
winbind	Using winbind.	Value: true/false

4.17 Samba Server

Configuration of a simple Samba server.

EXAMPLE 4.30: SAMBA SERVER CONFIGURATION

```
<samba-server>
  <accounts config:type="list"/>
  <backend/>
  <config config:type="list">
    <listentry>
      <name>global</name>
      <parameters>
        <security>domain</security>
        <usershare_allow_guests>No</usershare_allow_guests>
        <usershare_max_shares>100</usershare_max_shares>
        <workgroup>WORKGROUP</workgroup>
      </parameters>
    </listentry>
  </config>
```

```
    <service>Disabled</service>
    <trustdom/>
    <version>2.11</version>
  </samba-server>
```

Attribute	Values	Description
`accounts`	List of Samba accounts.	
`backend`	List of available Backends	Value: true/false
`config`	Setting additional user defined parameters in `/etc/samba/smb.conf`.	The example shows parameters in the `global` section of `/etc/samba/smb.conf`.
`service`	Samba service start during boot.	Value: Enabled/Disabled
`trustdom/`	Trusted Domains.	A map of two maps (keys: `establish, revoke`). Each map contains entries in the format key: domainname value: password.
`version`	Samba version	Default: 2.11

4.18 Authentication Client

The following is a simple example for an LDAP user authentication. NSS and PAM will automatically be configured accordingly. Required data are the name of the search base (base DN, e.g, `dc=mydomain,dc=com`) and the IP address of the LDAP server.

EXAMPLE 4.31: NETWORK CONFIGURATION: AUTHENTICATION CLIENT

```
<auth-client>
  <sssd>yes</sssd>
  <nssldap>no</nssldap>
```

```
  <sssd_conf>
    <sssd>
      <config_file_version>2</config_file_version>
      <services>nss, pam, sudo</services>
      <domains>EXAMPLE</domains>
    </sssd>
    <auth_domains>
      <domain>
        <domain_name>EXAMPLE</domain_name>
        <id_provider>ldap</id_provider>
        <sudo_provider>ldap</sudo_provider>
        <ldap_uri>ldap://example.com</ldap_uri>
        <ldap_sudo_search_base>ou=sudoers,dc=example,dc=com</ldap_sudo_search_base>
      </domain>
    </auth_domains>
  </sssd_conf>
</auth-client>
```

Tip: Using ldaps://

To use LDAP with native SSL (rather than TLS), add the `ldaps` resource:

```
<auth-client>
  <sssd_conf>
    <auth_domains>
      <domain>
        <ldaps config:type="boolean">true</ldaps>
      </domain>
    </auth_domains>
  </sssd_conf>
</auth-client>
```

4.19 NFS Client and Server

Configuring a system as an NFS client or an NFS server is can be done using the configuration system. The following examples show how both NFS client and server can be configured.

From SUSE Linux Enterprise 12 on, the structure of NFS client configuration has changed. Some global configuration options were introduced: `enable_nfs4` to switch NFS4 support on/off and `idmapd_domain` to define domain name for rpc.idmapd (this only makes sense when NFS4 is enabled). Attention: the old structure is not compatible with the new one and the control files with an NFS section created on older releases will not work with newer products.

EXAMPLE 4.32: NETWORK CONFIGURATION: NFS CLIENT

```
<nfs>
  <enable_nfs4 config:type="boolean">true</enable_nfs4>
  <idmapd_domain>suse.cz</idmapd_domain>
  <nfs_entries config:type="list">
    <nfs_entry>
      <mount_point>/home</mount_point>
      <nfs_options>sec=krb5i,intr,rw</nfs_options>
      <server_path>saurus.suse.cz:/home</server_path>
      <vfstype>nfs4</vfstype>
    </nfs_entry>
    <nfs_entry>
      <mount_point>/work</mount_point>
      <nfs_options>defaults</nfs_options>
      <server_path>bivoj.suse.cz:/work</server_path>
      <vfstype>nfs</vfstype>
    </nfs_entry>
    <nfs_entry>
      <mount_point>/mnt</mount_point>
      <nfs_options>defaults</nfs_options>
      <server_path>fallback.suse.cz:/srv/dist</server_path>
      <vfstype>nfs</vfstype>
    </nfs_entry>
  </nfs_entries>
</nfs>
```

EXAMPLE 4.33: NETWORK CONFIGURATION: NFS SERVER

```
<nfs_server>
  <nfs_exports config:type="list">
    <nfs_export>
      <allowed config:type="list">
        <allowed_clients>*(ro,root_squash,sync)</allowed_clients>
      </allowed>
      <mountpoint>/home</mountpoint>
    </nfs_export>
    <nfs_export>
      <allowed config:type="list">
        <allowed_clients>*(ro,root_squash,sync)</allowed_clients>
      </allowed>
      <mountpoint>/work</mountpoint>
    </nfs_export>
  </nfs_exports>
  <start_nfsserver config:type="boolean">true</start_nfsserver>
</nfs_server>
```

4.20 NTP Client

Select whether to start the NTP daemon when booting the system. The NTP daemon resolves host names when initializing.

To run NTP daemon in chroot jail, set `start_in_chroot`. Starting any daemon in a chroot jail is more secure and strongly recommended. To adjust NTP servers, peers, local clocks, and NTP broadcasting, add the appropriate entry to the control file. An example of various configuration options is shown below.

EXAMPLE 4.34: NETWORK CONFIGURATION: NTP CLIENT

```
<ntp-client>
  <configure_dhcp config:type="boolean">false</configure_dhcp>
  <peers config:type="list">
    <peer>
      <address>ntp.example.com</address>
      <options></options>
```

```
      <type>server</type>
    </peer>
  </peers>
  <start_at_boot config:type="boolean">true</start_at_boot>
  <start_in_chroot config:type="boolean">true</start_in_chroot>
</ntp-client>
```

4.21 Mail Configuration

For the mail configuration of the client, this module lets you create a detailed mail configuration. The module contains various options. We recommended you use it at least for the initial configuration.

EXAMPLE 4.35: MAIL CONFIGURATION

```
<mail>
  <aliases config:type="list">
    <alias>
      <alias>root</alias>
      <comment></comment>
      <destinations>foo</destinations>
    </alias>
    <alias>
      <alias>test</alias>
      <comment></comment>
      <destinations>foo</destinations>
    </alias>
  </aliases>
  <connection_type config:type="symbol">permanent</connection_type>
  <fetchmail config:type="list">
    <fetchmail_entry>
      <local_user>foo</local_user>
      <password>bar</password>
      <protocol>POP3</protocol>
      <remote_user>foo</remote_user>
      <server>pop.foo.com</server>
```

```
    </fetchmail_entry>
    <fetchmail_entry>
      <local_user>test</local_user>
      <password>bar</password>
      <protocol>IMAP</protocol>
      <remote_user>test</remote_user>
      <server>blah.com</server>
    </fetchmail_entry>
  </fetchmail>
  <from_header>test.com</from_header>
  <listen_remote config:type="boolean">true</listen_remote>
  <local_domains config:type="list">
    <domains>test1.com</domains>
  </local_domains>
  <masquerade_other_domains config:type="list">
      <domain>blah.com</domain>
  </masquerade_other_domains>
  <masquerade_users config:type="list">
    <masquerade_user>
      <address>joe@test.com</address>
      <comment></comment>
      <user>joeuser</user>
    </masquerade_user>
    <masquerade_user>
      <address>bar@test.com</address>
      <comment></comment>
      <user>foo</user>
    </masquerade_user>
  </masquerade_users>
  <mta config:type="symbol">postfix</mta>
  <outgoing_mail_server>test.com</outgoing_mail_server>
  <postfix_mda config:type="symbol">local</postfix_mda>
  <smtp_auth config:type="list">
    <listentry>
      <password>bar</password>
      <server>test.com</server>
```

```
      <user>foo</user>
    </listentry>
  </smtp_auth>
  <use_amavis config:type="boolean">true</use_amavis>
  <virtual_users config:type="list">
    <virtual_user>
      <alias>test.com</alias>
      <comment></comment>
      <destinations>foo.com</destinations>
    </virtual_user>
    <virtual_user>
      <alias>geek.com</alias>
      <comment></comment>
      <destinations>bar.com</destinations>
    </virtual_user>
  </virtual_users>
</mail>
```

4.22 Http Server Configuration

This section is used for configuration of an Apache http server.

For not so experienced users we would suggest to configure the Apache server via the `HTTP server` YAST module. After that he should call the `AutoYaST configuration` module, select the `HTTP server` YAST module and clone the Apache settings. These settings can be exported via the menu `File`.

EXAMPLE 4.36: HTTP SERVER CONFIGURATION

```
<http-server>
  <Listen config:type="list">
    <listentry>
      <ADDRESS/>
      <PORT>80</PORT>
    </listentry>
  </Listen>
  <hosts config:type="list">
```

```
<hosts_entry>
  <KEY>main</KEY>
  <VALUE config:type="list">
    <listentry>
      <KEY>DocumentRoot</KEY>
      <OVERHEAD>
      #
      # Global configuration that will be applicable for all
      # virtual hosts, unless deleted here, or overriden elswhere.
      #
      </OVERHEAD>
      <VALUE>"/srv/www/htdocs"</VALUE>
    </listentry>
    <listentry>
      <KEY>_SECTION</KEY>
      <OVERHEAD>
      #
      # Configure the DocumentRoot
      #
      </OVERHEAD>
      <SECTIONNAME>Directory</SECTIONNAME>
      <SECTIONPARAM>"/srv/www/htdocs"</SECTIONPARAM>
      <VALUE config:type="list">
        <listentry>
          <KEY>Options</KEY>
          <OVERHEAD>
          # Possible values for the Options directive are "None", "All",
          # or any combination of:
          #   Indexes Includes FollowSymLinks SymLinksifOwnerMatch
          #   ExecCGI MultiViews
          #
          # Note that "MultiViews" must be named *explicitly*
          # --- "Options All"
          # doesn't give it to you.
          #
          # The Options directive is both complicated and important.
```

```
# Please see
# http://httpd.apache.org/docs/2.4/mod/core.html#options
# for more information.
</OVERHEAD>
<VALUE>None</VALUE>
</listentry>
<listentry>
<KEY>AllowOverride</KEY>
<OVERHEAD>
# AllowOverride controls what directives may be placed in
# .htaccess files. It can be "All", "None", or any combination
# of the keywords:
#   Options FileInfo AuthConfig Limit
</OVERHEAD>
<VALUE>None</VALUE>
</listentry>
<listentry>
<KEY>_SECTION</KEY>
<OVERHEAD>
# Controls who can get stuff from this server.
</OVERHEAD>
<SECTIONNAME>IfModule</SECTIONNAME>
<SECTIONPARAM>!mod_access_compat.c</SECTIONPARAM>
<VALUE config:type="list">
  <listentry>
    <KEY>Require</KEY>
    <VALUE>all granted</VALUE>
  </listentry>
</VALUE>
</listentry>
<listentry>
<KEY>_SECTION</KEY>
<SECTIONNAME>IfModule</SECTIONNAME>
<SECTIONPARAM>mod_access_compat.c</SECTIONPARAM>
<VALUE config:type="list">
  <listentry>
```

```
            <KEY>Order</KEY>
            <VALUE>allow,deny</VALUE>
          </listentry>
          <listentry>
            <KEY>Allow</KEY>
            <VALUE>from all</VALUE>
          </listentry>
        </VALUE>
      </listentry>
    </VALUE>
  </listentry>
  <listentry>
    <KEY>Alias</KEY>
    <OVERHEAD>
    # Aliases: aliases can be added as needed (with no limit).
    # The format is Alias fakename realname
    #
    # Note that if you include a trailing / on fakename then the
    # server will require it to be present in the URL.  So "/icons"
    # isn't aliased in this example, only "/icons/".  If the fakename
    # is slash-terminated, then the realname must also be slash
    # terminated, and if the fakename omits the trailing slash, the
    # realname must also omit it.
    # We include the /icons/ alias for FancyIndexed directory listings.
    # If you do not use FancyIndexing, you may comment this out.
    #
    </OVERHEAD>
    <VALUE>/icons/ "/usr/share/apache2/icons/"</VALUE>
  </listentry>
  <listentry>
    <KEY>_SECTION</KEY>
    <OVERHEAD>
    </OVERHEAD>
    <SECTIONNAME>Directory</SECTIONNAME>
    <SECTIONPARAM>"/usr/share/apache2/icons"</SECTIONPARAM>
    <VALUE config:type="list">
```

```
        <listentry>
          <KEY>Options</KEY>
          <VALUE>Indexes MultiViews</VALUE>
        </listentry>
        <listentry>
          <KEY>AllowOverride</KEY>
          <VALUE>None</VALUE>
        </listentry>
        <listentry>
          <KEY>_SECTION</KEY>
          <SECTIONNAME>IfModule</SECTIONNAME>
          <SECTIONPARAM>!mod_access_compat.c</SECTIONPARAM>
          <VALUE config:type="list">
            <listentry>
              <KEY>Require</KEY>
              <VALUE>all granted</VALUE>
            </listentry>
          </VALUE>
        </listentry>
        <listentry>
          <KEY>_SECTION</KEY>
          <SECTIONNAME>IfModule</SECTIONNAME>
          <SECTIONPARAM>mod_access_compat.c</SECTIONPARAM>
          <VALUE config:type="list">
            <listentry>
              <KEY>Order</KEY>
              <VALUE>allow,deny</VALUE>
            </listentry>
            <listentry>
              <KEY>Allow</KEY>
              <VALUE>from all</VALUE>
            </listentry>
          </VALUE>
        </listentry>
      </VALUE>
    </listentry>
```

```
<listentry>
  <KEY>ScriptAlias</KEY>
  <OVERHEAD>
  # ScriptAlias: This controls which directories contain server
  # scripts. ScriptAliases are essentially the same as Aliases,
  # except that documents in the realname directory are treated
  # as applications and run by the server when requested rather
  # than as documents sent to the client.
  # The same rules about trailing "/" apply to ScriptAlias
  # directives as to Alias.
  #
  </OVERHEAD>
  <VALUE>/cgi-bin/ "/srv/www/cgi-bin/"</VALUE>
</listentry>
<listentry>
  <KEY>_SECTION</KEY>
  <OVERHEAD>
  # "/srv/www/cgi-bin" should be changed to whatever your
  # ScriptAliased CGI directory exists, if you have that configured.
  #
  </OVERHEAD>
  <SECTIONNAME>Directory</SECTIONNAME>
  <SECTIONPARAM>"/srv/www/cgi-bin"</SECTIONPARAM>
  <VALUE config:type="list">
    <listentry>
      <KEY>AllowOverride</KEY>
      <VALUE>None</VALUE>
    </listentry>
    <listentry>
      <KEY>Options</KEY>
      <VALUE>+ExecCGI -Includes</VALUE>
    </listentry>
    <listentry>
      <KEY>_SECTION</KEY>
      <SECTIONNAME>IfModule</SECTIONNAME>
      <SECTIONPARAM>!mod_access_compat.c</SECTIONPARAM>
```

```
        <VALUE config:type="list">
          <listentry>
            <KEY>Require</KEY>
            <VALUE>all granted</VALUE>
          </listentry>
        </VALUE>
      </listentry>
      <listentry>
        <KEY>_SECTION</KEY>
        <SECTIONNAME>IfModule</SECTIONNAME>
        <SECTIONPARAM>mod_access_compat.c</SECTIONPARAM>
        <VALUE config:type="list">
          <listentry>
            <KEY>Order</KEY>
            <VALUE>allow,deny</VALUE>
          </listentry>
          <listentry>
            <KEY>Allow</KEY>
            <VALUE>from all</VALUE>
          </listentry>
        </VALUE>
      </listentry>
    </VALUE>
  </listentry>
  <listentry>
    <KEY>_SECTION</KEY>
    <OVERHEAD>
    # UserDir: The name of the directory that is appended onto a
    # user's home directory if a ~user request is received.
    # To disable it, simply remove userdir from the list of modules
    # in APACHE_MODULES in /etc/sysconfig/apache2.
    #
    </OVERHEAD>
    <SECTIONNAME>IfModule</SECTIONNAME>
    <SECTIONPARAM>mod_userdir.c</SECTIONPARAM>
    <VALUE config:type="list">
```

```
      <listentry>
        <KEY>UserDir</KEY>
        <OVERHEAD>
        # Note that the name of the user directory ("public_html")
        # cannot simply be changed here, since it is a compile time
        # setting. The apache package would have to be rebuilt.
        # You could work around by deleting /usr/sbin/suexec, but
        # then all scripts from the directories would be executed
        # with the UID of the webserver.
        </OVERHEAD>
        <VALUE>public_html</VALUE>
      </listentry>
      <listentry>
        <KEY>Include</KEY>
        <OVERHEAD>
        # The actual configuration of the directory is in
        # /etc/apache2/mod_userdir.conf.
        </OVERHEAD>
        <VALUE>/etc/apache2/mod_userdir.conf</VALUE>
      </listentry>
    </VALUE>
  </listentry>
  <listentry>
    <KEY>IncludeOptional</KEY>
    <OVERHEAD>
    # Include all *.conf files from /etc/apache2/conf.d/.
    #
    # This is mostly meant as a place for other RPM packages to drop
    # in their configuration snippet.
    #
    # You can comment this out here if you want those bits include
    # only in a certain virtual host, but not here.
    #
    </OVERHEAD>
    <VALUE>/etc/apache2/conf.d/*.conf</VALUE>
  </listentry>
```

```
        <listentry>
          <KEY>IncludeOptional</KEY>
          <OVERHEAD>
          # The manual... if it is installed ('?' means it won't complain)
          </OVERHEAD>
          <VALUE>/etc/apache2/conf.d/apache2-manual?conf</VALUE>
        </listentry>
        <listentry>
          <KEY>ServerName</KEY>
          <VALUE>linux-wtyj</VALUE>
        </listentry>
        <listentry>
          <KEY>ServerAdmin</KEY>
          <OVERHEAD>
          </OVERHEAD>
          <VALUE>root@linux-wtyj</VALUE>
        </listentry>
        <listentry>
          <KEY>NameVirtualHost</KEY>
          <VALUE>192.168.43.2</VALUE>
        </listentry>
      </VALUE>
    </hosts_entry>
    <hosts_entry>
      <KEY>192.168.43.2/secondserver.suse.de</KEY>
      <VALUE config:type="list">
        <listentry>
          <KEY>DocumentRoot</KEY>
          <VALUE>/srv/www/htdocs</VALUE>
        </listentry>
        <listentry>
          <KEY>ServerName</KEY>
          <VALUE>secondserver.suse.de</VALUE>
        </listentry>
        <listentry>
          <KEY>ServerAdmin</KEY>
```

```
        <VALUE>second_server@suse.de</VALUE>
      </listentry>
      <listentry>
        <KEY>_SECTION</KEY>
        <SECTIONNAME>Directory</SECTIONNAME>
        <SECTIONPARAM>/srv/www/htdocs</SECTIONPARAM>
        <VALUE config:type="list">
          <listentry>
            <KEY>AllowOverride</KEY>
            <VALUE>None</VALUE>
          </listentry>
          <listentry>
            <KEY>Require</KEY>
            <VALUE>all granted</VALUE>
          </listentry>
        </VALUE>
      </listentry>
    </VALUE>
  </hosts_entry>
</hosts>
<modules config:type="list">
  <module_entry>
    <change>enable</change>
    <name>socache_shmcb</name>
    <userdefined config:type="boolean">true</userdefined>
  </module_entry>
  <module_entry>
    <change>enable</change>
    <name>reqtimeout</name>
    <userdefined config:type="boolean">true</userdefined>
  </module_entry>
  <module_entry>
    <change>enable</change>
    <name>authn_core</name>
    <userdefined config:type="boolean">true</userdefined>
  </module_entry>
```

```
    <module_entry>
      <change>enable</change>
      <name>authz_core</name>
      <userdefined config:type="boolean">true</userdefined>
    </module_entry>
  </modules>
  <service config:type="boolean">true</service>
  <version>2.9</version>
</http-server>
```

List Name	List Elements	Description
Listen		List of host `Listen` settings
	PORT	port address
	ADDRESS	Network address. All addresses will be taken if this entry is empty.
hosts		List of Hosts configuration
	KEY	Hostname; `<KEY>main</KEY>` defines the main hosts. e.g. `<KEY>192.168.43.2/secondserver.suse.de</KEY>`
	VALUE	List of diffent values which are describing the host.
modules		Module list. Only user defined modules have to be described.
	name	Modulename
	userdefined	Due historically reason it is always set to `true`.

List Name	List Elements	Description
	change	Due historically reason it is always set to `enable`.

Element	Description	Comment
version	Version of used Apache server	Just for information. Default 2.9
service	Enable Apache service	Optional. Default: false

Note: Firewall

A proper Firewall setting will be required to run the Apache server correctly.

4.23 SQUID Server

Squid is a caching and forwarding web proxy.

EXAMPLE 4.37: SQUID SERVER CONFIGURATION

```
<squid>
  <acls config:type="list">
    <listentry>
      <name>QUERY</name>
      <options config:type="list">
        <option>cgi-bin \?</option>
      </options>
      <type>urlpath_regex</type>
    </listentry>
    <listentry>
      <name>apache</name>
      <options config:type="list">
        <option>Server</option>
        <option>^Apache</option>
      </options>
```

```
      <type>rep_header</type>
    </listentry>
    <listentry>
      <name>all</name>
      <options config:type="list">
        <option>0.0.0.0/0.0.0.0</option>
      </options>
      <type>src</type>
    </listentry>
    <listentry>
      <name>manager</name>
      <options config:type="list">
        <option>cache_object</option>
      </options>
      <type>proto</type>
    </listentry>
    <listentry>
      <name>localhost</name>
      <options config:type="list">
        <option>127.0.0.1/255.255.255.255</option>
      </options>
      <type>src</type>
    </listentry>
    <listentry>
      <name>to_localhost</name>
      <options config:type="list">
        <option>127.0.0.0/8</option>
      </options>
      <type>dst</type>
    </listentry>
    <listentry>
      <name>SSL_ports</name>
      <options config:type="list">
        <option>443</option>
      </options>
      <type>port</type>
```

```
</listentry>
<listentry>
  <name>Safe_ports</name>
  <options config:type="list">
    <option>80</option>
  </options>
  <type>port</type>
</listentry>
<listentry>
  <name>Safe_ports</name>
  <options config:type="list">
    <option>21</option>
  </options>
  <type>port</type>
</listentry>
<listentry>
  <name>Safe_ports</name>
  <options config:type="list">
    <option>443</option>
  </options>
  <type>port</type>
</listentry>
<listentry>
  <name>Safe_ports</name>
  <options config:type="list">
    <option>70</option>
  </options>
  <type>port</type>
</listentry>
<listentry>
  <name>Safe_ports</name>
  <options config:type="list">
    <option>210</option>
  </options>
  <type>port</type>
</listentry>
```

```
<listentry>
  <name>Safe_ports</name>
  <options config:type="list">
    <option>1025-65535</option>
  </options>
  <type>port</type>
</listentry>
<listentry>
  <name>Safe_ports</name>
  <options config:type="list">
    <option>280</option>
  </options>
  <type>port</type>
</listentry>
<listentry>
  <name>Safe_ports</name>
  <options config:type="list">
    <option>488</option>
  </options>
  <type>port</type>
</listentry>
<listentry>
  <name>Safe_ports</name>
  <options config:type="list">
    <option>591</option>
  </options>
  <type>port</type>
</listentry>
<listentry>
  <name>Safe_ports</name>
  <options config:type="list">
    <option>777</option>
  </options>
  <type>port</type>
</listentry>
<listentry>
```

```
    <name>CONNECT</name>
    <options config:type="list">
      <option>CONNECT</option>
    </options>
    <type>method</type>
  </listentry>
</acls>
<http_accesses config:type="list">
  <listentry>
    <acl config:type="list">
      <listentry>manager</listentry>
      <listentry>localhost</listentry>
    </acl>
    <allow config:type="boolean">true</allow>
  </listentry>
  <listentry>
    <acl config:type="list">
      <listentry>manager</listentry>
    </acl>
    <allow config:type="boolean">false</allow>
  </listentry>
  <listentry>
    <acl config:type="list">
      <listentry>!Safe_ports</listentry>
    </acl>
    <allow config:type="boolean">false</allow>
  </listentry>
  <listentry>
    <acl config:type="list">
      <listentry>CONNECT</listentry>
      <listentry>!SSL_ports</listentry>
    </acl>
    <allow config:type="boolean">false</allow>
  </listentry>
  <listentry>
    <acl config:type="list">
```

```
        <listentry>localhost</listentry>
      </acl>
      <allow config:type="boolean">true</allow>
    </listentry>
    <listentry>
      <acl config:type="list">
        <listentry>all</listentry>
      </acl>
      <allow config:type="boolean">false</allow>
    </listentry>
  </http_accesses>
  <http_ports config:type="list">
    <listentry>
      <host/>
      <port>3128</port>
      <transparent config:type="boolean">false</transparent>
    </listentry>
  </http_ports>
  <refresh_patterns config:type="list">
    <listentry>
      <case_sensitive config:type="boolean">true</case_sensitive>
      <max>10080</max>
      <min>1440</min>
      <percent>20</percent>
      <regexp>^ftp:</regexp>
    </listentry>
    <listentry>
      <case_sensitive config:type="boolean">true</case_sensitive>
      <max>1440</max>
      <min>1440</min>
      <percent>0</percent>
      <regexp>^gopher:</regexp>
    </listentry>
    <listentry>
      <case_sensitive config:type="boolean">true</case_sensitive>
      <max>4320</max>
```

```
        <min>0</min>
        <percent>20</percent>
        <regexp>.</regexp>
      </listentry>
    </refresh_patterns>
    <service_enabled_on_startup config:type="boolean">true</
service_enabled_on_startup>
    <settings>
      <access_log config:type="list">
        <listentry>/var/log/squid/access.log</listentry>
      </access_log>
      <cache_dir config:type="list">
        <listentry>ufs</listentry>
        <listentry>/var/cache/squid</listentry>
        <listentry>100</listentry>
        <listentry>16</listentry>
        <listentry>256</listentry>
      </cache_dir>
      <cache_log config:type="list">
        <listentry>/var/log/squid/cache.log</listentry>
      </cache_log>
      <cache_mem config:type="list">
        <listentry>8</listentry>
        <listentry>MB</listentry>
      </cache_mem>
      <cache_mgr config:type="list">
        <listentry>webmaster</listentry>
      </cache_mgr>
      <cache_replacement_policy config:type="list">
        <listentry>lru</listentry>
      </cache_replacement_policy>
      <cache_store_log config:type="list">
        <listentry>/var/log/squid/store.log</listentry>
      </cache_store_log>
      <cache_swap_high config:type="list">
        <listentry>95</listentry>
```

```
      </cache_swap_high>
      <cache_swap_low config:type="list">
        <listentry>90</listentry>
      </cache_swap_low>
      <client_lifetime config:type="list">
        <listentry>1</listentry>
        <listentry>days</listentry>
      </client_lifetime>
      <connect_timeout config:type="list">
        <listentry>2</listentry>
        <listentry>minutes</listentry>
      </connect_timeout>
      <emulate_httpd_log config:type="list">
        <listentry>off</listentry>
      </emulate_httpd_log>
      <error_directory config:type="list">
        <listentry/>
      </error_directory>
      <ftp_passive config:type="list">
        <listentry>on</listentry>
      </ftp_passive>
      <maximum_object_size config:type="list">
        <listentry>4096</listentry>
        <listentry>KB</listentry>
      </maximum_object_size>
      <memory_replacement_policy config:type="list">
        <listentry>lru</listentry>
      </memory_replacement_policy>
      <minimum_object_size config:type="list">
        <listentry>0</listentry>
        <listentry>KB</listentry>
      </minimum_object_size>
    </settings>
  </squid>
```

Attribute	Values	Description
`acls`	List of Access Control Settings (ACLs).	Each list entry contains the name, type and an additional options. Use the YAST Squid configuration module in order to get an overview about possible entries.
`http_accesses`	In the Access Control table, access can be denied or allowed to ACL Groups.	If there are more ACL Groups in one definition, it means that access will be allowed or denied to members who belong to all ACL Groups at the same time. The Access Control table is checked in the order listed here. The first matching entry is used.
`http_ports`	Define all ports where Squid will listen for clients' http requests.	`Host` can contain a hostname or IP address or remain empty. `transparent` disable PMTU discovery when transparent.
`refresh_patterns`	Refresh Patterns define how Squid treats the objects in the cache.	The refresh patterns are checked in the order listed here. The first matching entry is used. `Min` determines how long (in minutes) an object should be considered fresh if no explicit expiry time is given. `Max` is the upper limit of how long objects without an explicit

Attribute	Values	Description
		expiry time will be considered fresh. `Percent` is the percentage of the object's age (time since last modification). An object without explicit expiry time will be considered fresh.
`settings`	Map of all available general parameters with defalut values.	Use the YAST Squid configuration module in order to get an overview about possible entries.
`service_enabled_on_startup`	SQUID service start when booting.	Value: true/false

4.24 FTP Server

Configure your FTP Internet server settings.

EXAMPLE 4.38: FTP SERVER CONFIGURATION:

```
<ftp-server>
  <AnonAuthen>1</AnonAuthen>
  <AnonCreatDirs>NO</AnonCreatDirs>
  <AnonMaxRate>0</AnonMaxRate>
  <AnonReadOnly>YES</AnonReadOnly>
  <AntiWarez>YES</AntiWarez>
  <Banner>Welcome message</Banner>
  <CertFile/>
  <ChrootEnable>NO</ChrootEnable>
  <EnableUpload>NO</EnableUpload>
  <FTPUser>ftp</FTPUser>
  <FtpDirAnon>/srv/ftp</FtpDirAnon>
  <FtpDirLocal/>
```

```
    <GuestUser/>
    <LocalMaxRate>0</LocalMaxRate>
    <MaxClientsNumber>10</MaxClientsNumber>
    <MaxClientsPerIP>3</MaxClientsPerIP>
    <MaxIdleTime>15</MaxIdleTime>
    <PasMaxPort>40500</PasMaxPort>
    <PasMinPort>40000</PasMinPort>
    <PassiveMode>YES</PassiveMode>
    <SSL>0</SSL>
    <SSLEnable>NO</SSLEnable>
    <SSLv2>NO</SSLv2>
    <SSLv3>NO</SSLv3>
    <StartDaemon>0</StartDaemon>
    <TLS>YES</TLS>
    <Umask/>
    <UmaskAnon/>
    <UmaskLocal/>
    <VerboseLogging>NO</VerboseLogging>
    <VirtualUser>NO</VirtualUser>
  </ftp-server>
```

Element	Description	Comment
AnonAuthen	Enable/Disable Anonymous and Local Users.	Authenticated Users Only: 1; Anonymous Only: 0; Both: 2
AnonCreatDirs	Anonymous can create dirs.	Values: YES/NO
AnonReadOnly	Anonymous Can Upload	Values: YES/NO
AnonMaxRate	The maximum data transfer rate permitted for anonymous clients.	KB/s

Element	Description	Comment
AntiWarez	Disallow downloading of files that were uploaded but not validated by a local admin.	Values: YES/NO
Banner	Specify the name of a file containing the text to display when someone connects to the server.	
CertFile	DSA Certificate to Use for SSL-encrypted Connections	This option specifies the location of the DSA certificate to use for SSL-encrypted connections.
ChrootEnable	When enabled, local users will be (by default) placed in a chroot() jail in their home directory after login.	Warning: This option has security implications. Values: YES/NO
EnableUpload	If enabled, FTP users can upload.	To allow anonymous users to upload, enable `AnonReadOnly`. Values: YES/NO
FTPUser	Defining anonymous FTP user.	
FtpDirAnon	FTP Directory for Anonymous Users.	Specify a directory which is used for FTP anonymous users.
FtpDirLocal	FTP Directory for Authenticated Users.	Specify a directory which is used for FTP authenticated users.

Element	Description	Comment
LocalMaxRate	The maximum data transfer rate permitted for local authenticated users.	KB/s
MaxClientsNumber	The maximum number of clients allowed to connect.	
MaxClientsPerIP	Max Clients for One IP.	The maximum number of clients allowed to connect from the same source internet address.
MaxIdleTime	The maximum time (timeout) a remote client may wait between FTP commands.	Minutes
PasMaxPort	Maximum value for a port range for passive connection replies.	`PassiveMode` has to be set to YES.
PasMinPort	Minimal value for a port range for passive connection replies.	`PassiveMode` has to be set to YES.
PassiveMode	Enable Passive Mode	Value: YES/NO
SSL	Security Settings	Disable SSL/TLS: 0; Accept SSL and TLS: 1; Refuse Connections Without SSL/TLS: 2
SSLEnable	If enabled, SSL connections are allowed.	Value: YES/NO
SSLv2	If enabled, SSL version 2 connections are allowed.	Value: YES/NO

Element	Description	Comment
SSLv3	If enabled, SSL version 3 connections are allowed.	Value: YES/NO
StartDaemon	FTP deamon ist started.	manually: 0; when booting: 1; via xinetd: 2
TLS	If enabled, TLS connections are allowed.	Value: YES/NO
Umask	File creation mask. (umask for files):(umask for dirs).	E.g. 177:077 if you feel paranoid.
UmaskAnon	The value to which the umask for file creation is set for anonymous users.	If you want to specify octal values, remember the "0" prefix, otherwise the value will be treated as a base 10 integer.
UmaskLocal	Umask for Authenticated Users.	If you want to specify octal values, remember the "0" prefix, otherwise the value will be treated as a base 10 integer.
VerboseLogging	When enabled, all FTP requests and responses are logged.	Value: YES/NO
VirtualUser	By using virtual users, FTP accounts can be administrated without affecting system accounts.	Value: YES/NO

Note: Firewall

A proper Firewall setting will be required to run the Ftp server correctly.

4.25 TFTP Server

Configure your TFTP Internet server settings.

Use this to enable a server for TFTP (trivial file transfer protocol). The server will be started using xinetd.

Note that TFTP and FTP are not the same.

EXAMPLE 4.39: TFTP SERVER CONFIGURATION:

```
<tftp-server>
  <start_tftpd config:type="boolean">true</start_tftpd>
  <tftp_directory>/tftpboot</tftp_directory>
</tftp-server>
```

Element	Description	Comment
start_tftpd	Enabling TFTP server service.	Value: true/false
tftp_directory	Boot Image Directory: Specify the directory where served files are located.	The usual value is /tftpboot. The directory will be created if it does not exist. The server uses this as its root directory (using the -s option).

4.26 Firstboot Workflow

The YaST firstboot utility (YaST Initial System Configuration), which runs after the installation is completed, lets you configure the before creation of the install image so that on the first boot after configuration, users are guided through a series of steps that allow for easier configuration of their desktops. YaST firstboot does not run by default and has to be configured to run.

EXAMPLE 4.40: ENABELING FIRSTBOOT WORKFLOW

```
<firstboot>
  <firstboot_enabled config:type="boolean">true</firstboot_enabled>
</firstboot>
```

4.27 Security Settings

Using the features of this module, you can to change the local security settings on the target system. The local security settings include the boot configuration, login settings, password settings, user addition settings, and file permissions.

Configuring the security settings automatically corresponds to the `Custom Settings` in the security module available in the running system which lets you create your own, customized configuration.

EXAMPLE 4.41: SECURITY CONFIGURATION

See the reference for the meaning and the possible values of the settings in the following example.

```
<security>
  <console_shutdown>ignore</console_shutdown>
  <cwd_in_root_path>no</cwd_in_root_path>
  <displaymanager_remote_access>no</displaymanager_remote_access>
  <fail_delay>3</fail_delay>
  <faillog_enab>yes</faillog_enab>
  <gid_max>60000</gid_max>
  <gid_min>101</gid_min>
  <gdm_shutdown>root</gdm_shutdown>
  <lastlog_enab>yes</lastlog_enab>
  <encryption>md5</encryption>
  <obscure_checks_enab>no</obscure_checks_enab>
  <pass_max_days>99999</pass_max_days>
  <pass_max_len>8</pass_max_len>
  <pass_min_days>1</pass_min_days>
  <pass_min_len>6</pass_min_len>
  <pass_warn_age>14</pass_warn_age>
  <passwd_use_cracklib>yes</passwd_use_cracklib>
  <permission_security>secure</permission_security>
  <run_updatedb_as>nobody</run_updatedb_as>
  <uid_max>60000</uid_max>
```

```
  <uid_min>500</uid_min>
</security>
```

4.27.1 Password Settings Options

Change various password settings. These settings are mainly stored in the `/etc/login.defs` file.

Use this resource to activate one of the encryption methods currently supported. If not set, `DES` is configured.

`DES`, the Linux default method, works in all network environments, but it restricts you to passwords no longer than eight characters. `MD5` allows longer passwords, thus provides more security, but some network protocols do not support this, and you may have problems with NIS. `Blowfish` is also supported.

Additionally, you can set up the system to check for password plausibility and length etc.

4.27.2 Boot Settings

Use the security resource, to change various boot settings.

How to interpret Ctrl–Alt–Del?

When someone at the console has pressed the Ctrl–Alt–Del key combination, the system usually reboots. Sometimes it is desirable to ignore this event, for example, when the system serves as both workstation and server.

Shutdown behavior of GDM

Configure a list of users allowed to shut down the machine from GDM.

4.27.3 Login Settings

Change various login settings. These settings are mainly stored in the `/etc/login.defs` file.

4.27.4 New user settings (`useradd` settings)

Set the minimum and maximum possible user and group ID

4.28 Linux Audit Framework (LAF)

This module allows the configuration of the audit daemon as well as to add rules for the audit subsystem.

EXAMPLE 4.42: LAF CONFIGURATION

```
<audit-laf>
  <auditd>
    <flush>INCREMENTAL</flush>
    <freq>20</freq>
    <log_file>/var/log/audit/audit.log</log_file>
    <log_format>RAW</log_format>
    <max_log_file>5</max_log_file>
    <max_log_file_action>ROTATE</max_log_file_action>
    <name_format>NONE</name_format>
    <num_logs>4</num_logs>
  </auditd>
  <rules/>
</audit-laf>
```

Attribute	Values	Description
`auditd/flush`	Describes how to write the data to disk.	If set to `INCREMENTAL` the Frequency parameter tells how many records to write before issuing an explicit flush to disk. `NONE` means: no special effort is made to flush data, `DATA`: keep data portion synced, `SYNC`: keep data and meta-data fully synced.
`auditd/freq`	This parameter tells how many records to write before issuing an explicit flush to disk.	The parameter `flush` has to be set to `INCREMENTAL`.

Attribute	Values	Description
auditd/log_file	The full path name to the log file.	
auditd/log_fomat	How much information has to be logged.	Set RAW to log all data (store in a format exactly as the kernel sends it) or NOLOG to discard all audit information instead of writing it on disk (does not affect data sent to the dispatcher).
auditd/max_log_file	How much information has to be logged.	Unit: Megabytes
auditd/num_logs	Number of log files.	max_log_file_action has to be set to ROTATE
au-ditd/max_log_file_action	What happens if the log capacity has been reached.	If the action is set to RO-TATE the Number of Log Files specifies the number of files to keep. Set to SYSLOG, the audit daemon will write a warning to /var/log/messages. With SUSPEND the daemon stops writing records to disk. IGNORE means do nothing, KEEP_LOGS is similar to ROTATE, but log files are not overwritten.
auditd/name_format	Computer Name Format describes how to write the computer name to the log file.	If USER is set, the User Defined Name is used. NONE means no computer name is inserted. HOSTNAME uses the name returned by the 'geth-

Attribute	Values	Description
		ostname' syscall. `FQD` uses the fully qualified domain name.
`rules`	Rules for auditctl	You can edit the rules manually, which we only recommended for advanced users. For more information about all options, see 'man auditctl'.

4.29 Users

The `root` and at least one normal user can be added during install using data supplied in the control file. User data and passwords (encrypted or in clear text) are part of the `configure` resource in the control file.

At least the `root` should be configured during auto-installation so you can login after the installation is finished. It will also ensure nobody else can login to the system (in case the password is not set).

The two users in the following example are added during system configuration.

EXAMPLE 4.43: USER CONFIGURATION

```
<users config:type="list">
  <user>
    <username>root</username>
    <user_password>password</user_password>
    <encrypted config:type="boolean">true</encrypted>
    <forename/>
    <surname/>
  </user>
  <user>
    <username>tux</username>
    <user_password>password</user_password>
    <encrypted config:type="boolean">true</encrypted>
```

```
    <forename>Tux</forename>
    <surname>Linux</surname>
  </user>
</users>
```

The last example shows the minimal information required for adding users. Additional options are available for a more customized user account management. The data in `/etc/default/useradd` is used to determine the home directory of the user to be created plus other parameters.

Note: Users set up during the first stage

Starting with SUSE Linux Enterprise Server 12 SP1, users are set up during the first stage (in previous versions it happened in the second one). So with a minimal profile, you can set up an usable system running only the first stage.

4.30 Custom User Scripts

By adding scripts to the auto-installation process you can customize the installation according to your needs and take control in different stages of the installation.

In the auto-installation process, five types of scripts can be executed at different points in time during the installation:

All scripts need to be in the <scritps> section.

- `pre-scripts` (very early, before anything else really happens)
- `postpartitioning-scripts` (after partitioning and mounting to `/mnt` but before RPM installation)
- `chroot-scripts` (after the package installation, before the first boot)
- `post-scripts` (during the first boot of the installed system, no services running)
- `init-scripts` (during the first boot of the installed system, all services up and running)

4.30.1 Pre-Install Scripts

Executed before YaST does any real change to the system (before partitioning and package installation but after the hardware detection).

You can use a pre-script to modify your control file and let AutoYaST reread it. Find your control file in `/tmp/profile/autoinst.xml`. Adjust the file and store the modified version in `/tmp/profile/modified.xml`. AutoYaST will read the modified file after the pre-script finishes.

It is also possible to change the partitioning in your pre-script.

Note: Pre-Install Scripts with Confirmation

Pre-scripts are executed at an early stage of the installation. This means if you have requested to confirm the installation, the pre-scripts will be executed before the confirmation screen shows up (`profile/install/general/mode/confirm`).

Note: Pre-Install and Zypper

If you would like to call *zypper* in the pre-install script you will have to set the environment variable *ZYPP_LOCKFILE_ROOT="/var/run/autoyast"* in order to prevent conflicts with the running YAST process.

Pre-Install Script elements must be placed as follows:

```
<scripts>
  <pre-scripts config:type="list">
    <script>
      ...
    </script>
  </pre-scripts>
</scripts>
```

4.30.2 Post-partitioning Scripts

Executed after YaST has done the partitioning and written the fstab. The empty system is already mounted to `/mnt`.

Post-partitioning script elements must be placed as follows:

```
<scripts>
  <postpartitioning-scripts config:type="list">
    <script>
      ...
    </script>
  </postpartitioning-scripts>
</scripts>
```

4.30.3 Chroot Environment Scripts

Chroot scripts are executed before the machine reboots for the first time. You can execute chroot scripts before the installation chroots into the installed system and configures the boot loader or you can execute a script after the chroot into the installed system has happened (look at the `chrooted` parameter for that).

Chroot Environment script elements must be placed as follows:

```
<scripts>
  <chroot-scripts config:type="list">
    <script>
      ...
    </script>
  </chroot-scripts>
</scripts>
```

4.30.4 Post-Install Scripts

These scripts are executed after AutoYaST has completed the system configuration and after it has booted the system for the first time.

It is possible to execute post scripts in an earlier phase while the installation network is still up and before AutoYaST configures the system. To run network-enabled post scripts, the boolean property `network_needed` needs to be set to `true`.

Post-install script elements must be placed as follows:

```
<scripts>
    <post-scripts config:type="list">
      <script>
        ...
      </script>
    </post-scripts>
  </scripts>
```

4.30.5 Init Scripts

These scripts are executed when YaST has finished, during the initial boot process after the network has been initialized. These final scripts are executed using `/usr/lib/YaST2/bin/autoyast-initscripts.sh` and are executed only once. Init scripts are configured using the tag *init-scripts*.

The following elements must be between the <scripts><init-scripts config:type="list"><script> ... </script></init-scripts>...</scripts> tags

TABLE 4.2: INIT SCRIPT XML REPRESENTATION

Element	Description	Comment
`location`	Define a location from where the script gets fetched. Locations can be the same as for the profile (HTTP, FTP, NFS, etc.). `<location >http://10.10.0.1/ myInitScript.sh</ location>`	Either <location> or <source> must be defined.
`source`	The script itself (source code), encapsulated in a CDATA tag. If you do not	Either <location> or <source> must be defined.

Element	Description	Comment

	want to put the whole shell script into the XML profile, use the location parameter.
	
	`<source>`
	`<![CDATA[`
	`echo "Testing the init script" > /tmp/init_out.txt`
	`]]>`
	`</source>`	

`filename`	The file name of the script. It will be stored in a temporary directory under `/tmp` `<filename>mynitScript5.sh</filename>`	Optional ion case you only have a single init script. The default name (`init-scripts`) is used in this case. If having specified more than one init script, you must set a unique name for each script.
`rerun`	A script is only run once. Even if you use ayast_setup to run an XML file multiple times, the script is only run once. Change this default behavior by setting this boolean to `true`. `<rerun config:type="boolean">true</rerun>`	Optional, default is `false` (scripts only run once).

When added to the control file manually, scripts need to be included in a *CDATA* element to avoid confusion with the file syntax and other tags defined in the control file.

4.30.6 Script XML Representation

All XML elements described below can be used for each of the script types described above. The only exceptions are `chrooted` and `network_needed`—they are only valid for chroot and post-install scripts.

TABLE 4.3: SCRIPT XML REPRESENTATION

Element	Description	Comment
`location`	Define a location from where the script gets fetched. Locations can be the same as for the control file (HTTP, FTP, NFS, etc.). <location >http://10.10.0.1/myPreScript.sh</ location>	Either `location` or `source` must be defined.
`source`	The script itself (source code), encapsulated in a CDATA tag. If you do not want to put the whole shell script into the XML control file, refer to the location parameter. <source> <![CDATA[echo "Testing the pre script" > /tmp/ pre-script_out.txt]]> </source>	Either `location` or `source` must be defined.
`inter-preter`	Specify the interpreter that must be used for the script. Supported options are shell and perl. <interpreter>perl</interpreter>	Optional (default is `shell`).
`file name`	The file name of the script. It will be stored in a temporary directory under `/tmp`.	Optional. Default is the type of the script (pre-scripts in this case). If you have more

Element	Description	Comment
	`<filename>myPreScript5.sh</filename>`	than one script, you should define different names for each script.
`feedback`	If this boolean is `true`, output and error messages of the script (STDOUT and STDERR) will be shown in a pop-up, which the user needs to confirm via the OK button. the pop-up will only be shown if the script produces any such output. `<feedback config:type="boolean">true</feedback>`	Optional, default is `false`.
`feedback_type`	This can be `message`, `warning` or `error`. Set the timeout for these pop-ups in the <report> section. `<feedback_type>warning</feedback_type>`	Optional, if missing, an always blocking pop-up is used.
`debug`	If this is `true`, every single line of a shell script is logged. Perl scripts are run with warnings turned on. `<debug config:type="boolean">true</debug>`	Optional, default is `true`.
`notification`	This text will be shown in a pop-up for the time the script is running in the background. `<notification>Please wait while script is running...</notification>`	Optional, if not configured, no notification pop-up will be shown.

Element	Description	Comment
`param-list`	It is possible to specify parameters given to the script being called. You may have more than one `param` entry. They are concatenated by a single space character on the script command line. If any shell quoting should be necessary (for example to protect embedded spaces) you need to include this. <param-list> <param>par1</param> <param>par2 par3</param> <param>"par4.1 par4.2"</param> </param-list>	Optional, if not configured, no parameters get passed to script.
`rerun`	A script is only run once. Even if you use `ayast`_setup to run an XML file multiple times, the script is only run once. Change this default behavior by setting this boolean to `true`. <rerun config:type="boolean">true</ rerun>	Optional, default is `false` (scripts only run once).
`chrooted`	If set to `false`, the installed system remains mounted at `/mnt` and no chroot happens. The boot loader is not installed either at this stage. Setting it to `true` means, a chroot into `/mnt` is performed, where the installed system is mounted. The boot loader is installed, and if you want to change anything in the installed system, you do not need to use the `/mnt` prefix anymore. <chrooted config:type="boolean"	Optional, default is `false`. This option is only available for chroot environment scripts.

Element	Description	Comment
	`>true</chrooted>`	
`network_needed`	If set to `false` the script will run after the YaST modules like the user configuration and everything else are done. The network is configured but not up and running yet. With this value set to `true`, the script runs before all YaST modules are configured. So there is no local user and no network is configured but the installation network is still up and running (if you did a network installation).. `<network_needed config:type="boolean" >true</network_needed>`	Optional, default is `false`. This option is only available for post-install scripts.

4.30.7 Script Example

EXAMPLE 4.44: SCRIPT CONFIGURATION

```
<?xml version="1.0"?>
<!DOCTYPE profile>
<profile xmlns="http://www.suse.com/1.0/yast2ns" xmlns:config="http://
www.suse.com/1.0/configns">
<scripts>
  <chroot-scripts config:type="list">
    <script>
      <chrooted config:type="boolean">true</chrooted>
      <filename>chroot.sh</filename>
      <interpreter>shell</interpreter>
      <source><![CDATA[
#!/bin/sh
echo "Testing chroot (chrooted) scripts"
ls
]]>
```

```
      </source>
    </script>
    <script>
      <filename>chroot.sh</filename>
        <interpreter>shell</interpreter>
        <source><![CDATA[
#!/bin/sh
echo "Testing chroot scripts"
df
cd /mnt
ls
]]>
        </source>
      </script>
    </chroot-scripts>
    <post-scripts config:type="list">
      <script>
        <filename>post.sh</filename>
        <interpreter>shell</interpreter>
        <source><![CDATA[
#!/bin/sh

echo "Running Post-install script"
systemctl start portmap
mount -a 192.168.1.1:/local /mnt
cp /mnt/test.sh /tmp
umount /mnt
]]>
        </source>
      </script>
      <script>
        <filename>post.pl</filename>
        <interpreter>perl</interpreter>
        <source><![CDATA[
#!/usr/bin/perl
print "Running Post-install script";
```

```
]]>
        </source>
      </script>
    </post-scripts>
    <pre-scripts config:type="list">
      <script>
        <interpreter>shell</interpreter>
        <location>http://192.168.1.1/profiles/scripts/prescripts.sh</location>
      </script>
      <script>
        <filename>pre.sh</filename>
        <interpreter>shell</interpreter>
        <source><![CDATA[
#!/bin/sh
echo "Running pre-install script"
]]>
        </source>
      </script>
    </pre-scripts>
    <postpartitioning-scripts config:type="list">
      <script>
        <filename>postpart.sh</filename>
        <interpreter>shell</interpreter>
        <debug config:type="boolean">false</debug>
        <feedback config:type="boolean">true</feedback>
        <source><![CDATA[
touch /mnt/testfile
echo Hi
]]>
        </source>
      </script>
    </postpartitioning-scripts>
  </scripts>
</profile>
```

After installation is finished, the scripts and the output logs can be found in the directory `/var/adm/autoinstall`. The scripts are located in the subdirectory `scripts` and the output logs in the `log` directory.

The log consists of the output produced when executing the shell scripts using the following command:

```
/bin/sh -x SCRIPT_NAME 2&>/var/adm/autoinstall/logs/SCRIPT_NAME.log
```

4.31 System Variables (Sysconfig)

Using the sysconfig resource, it is possible to define configuration variables in the sysconfig repository (`/etc/sysconfig`) directly. Sysconfig variables, offer the possibility to fine-tune many system components and environment variables exactly to your needs.

The following example shows how a variable can be set using the sysconfig resource.

EXAMPLE 4.45: SYSCONFIG CONFIGURATION

```
<sysconfig config:type="list" >
  <sysconfig_entry>
    <sysconfig_key>XNTPD_INITIAL_NTPDATE</sysconfig_key>
    <sysconfig_path>/etc/sysconfig/xntp</sysconfig_path>
    <sysconfig_value>ntp.host.com</sysconfig_value>
  </sysconfig_entry>
  <sysconfig_entry>
    <sysconfig_key>HTTP_PROXY</sysconfig_key>
    <sysconfig_path>/etc/sysconfig/proxy</sysconfig_path>
    <sysconfig_value>proxy.host.com:3128</sysconfig_value>
  </sysconfig_entry>
  <sysconfig_entry>
    <sysconfig_key>FTP_PROXY</sysconfig_key>
    <sysconfig_path>/etc/sysconfig/proxy</sysconfig_path>
    <sysconfig_value>proxy.host.com:3128</sysconfig_value>
  </sysconfig_entry>
</sysconfig>
```

Both relative and absolute paths can be provided. If no absolute path is given, it is treated as a sysconfig file under the `/etc/sysconfig` directory.

4.32 Adding Complete Configurations

For many applications and services you might have prepared a configuration file which should be copied to the appropriate location in the installed system, for example if you are installing a Web server and have a `ready to go` server configuration file (`httpd.conf`).

Using this resource, you can embed the file into the control file by specifying the final path on the installed system. YaST will copy this file to the specified location.

This feature requires the autoyast2 package to be installed. If the package is missing, AutoYaST will automatically install the package if it is missing.

You can specify the `file_location` where the file should be retrieved from. This can also be a location on the network such as an HTTP server: `<file_location>http://my.server.site/issue</file_location>`.

You can create directories by specifying a `file_path` that ends with a slash.

EXAMPLE 4.46: DUMPING FILES INTO THE INSTALLED SYSTEM

```
<files config:type="list">
  <file>
    <file_path>/etc/apache2/httpd.conf</file_path>
    <file_contents>

<![CDATA[
some content
]]>

    </file_contents>
  </file>
  <file>
    <file_path>/mydir/a/b/c/</file_path> <!-- create directory -->
  </file>
</files>
```

A more advanced example is shown below. This configuration will create a file using the content supplied in `file_contents` and change the permissions and ownership of the file. After the file has been copied to the system, a script is executed, which can be used to manipulate the file and prepare it for the environment of the client.

EXAMPLE 4.47: DUMPING FILES INTO THE INSTALLED SYSTEM

```
<files config:type="list">
  <file>
    <file_path>/etc/someconf.conf</file_path>
    <file_contents>

<![CDATA[
some content
]]>

    </file_contents>
    <file_owner>tux.users</file_owner>
    <file_permissions>444</file_permissions>
    <file_script>
      <interpreter>shell</interpreter>
      <source>

<![CDATA[
#!/bin/sh

echo "Testing file scripts" >> /etc/someconf.conf
df
cd /mnt
ls
]]>

      </source>
    </file_script>
  </file>
</files>
```

4.33 Ask the User for Values during Installation

You have the option to let the user decide the values of specific parts of the control file during the installation. If you use this feature, a pop-up will ask the user to enter a specific part of the control file during installation. If you want a full auto installation, but the user should set the password of the local account, you can do this via the `ask` directive in the control file.

The elements listed below must be placed within the following XML structure:

```
<general>
  <ask-list config:type="list">
    <ask>
      ...
    </ask>
  </ask-list> tags
</general>
```

TABLE 4.4: ASK THE USER FOR VALUES: XML REPRESENTATION

Element	Description	Comment
`question`	The question you want to ask the user. `<question>Enter the LDAP server</question>`	The default value is the path to the element (the path often looks strange, so we recommend entering a question).
`default`	Set a preselection for the user. A text entry will be filled out with this value. A check box will be true or false and a selection will have the given value preselected. `<default>dc=suse,dc=de</default>`	Optional.

Element	Description	Comment
help	An optional help text that is shown on the left side of the question. `<help>Enter the LDAP server address.</help>`	Optional.
title	An optional title that is shown above the questions. `<title>LDAP server</title>`	Optional.
type	The type of the element you want to change. Possible values are symbol, boolean, string and integer. The file system in the partition section is a symbol, while the encrypted element in the user configuration is a boolean. You can see the type of that element if you look in your control file at the config:type="...." attribute. You can also use static_text as type. A static_text is a text that does not require any user input and can be used to show information if it is not wanted in the help text. `<type>symbol</type>`	Optional. The default is string. If type is symbol, you must provide the selection element too (see below).

Element	Description	Comment
password	If this boolean is set to true, a password dialog pops up instead of a simple text entry. Setting this to true only makes sense if type is string. <password config:type="boolean">true</password>	Optional. The default is false.
pathlist	A list of path elements. A path is a comma separated list of elements that describes the path to the element you want to change. For example, the LDAP server element can be found in the control file in the <ldap> <ldap_server> section. So if you want to change that value, you need to set the path to ldap,ldap_server. If you want to change the password of the first user in the control file, you need to set the path to users,0,user_password. The 0 indicates the first user in the <users config:type="list"> list of users in the control file. <pathlist config:type="list">	This information is optional but you should at least provide path or file.

Element	Description	Comment

	`<path>networking,dns,hostname</path>`
	`<path>...</path>`
	`</pathlist>`	

`file`	You can store the answer to a question in a file, to use it in one of your scripts later. If you ask during `stage=inital` and you want to use the answer in stage2, then you need to copy the answer-file in a chroot script that is running as `chrooted=false`. Use the command: **`cp /tmp/my_answer /mnt/tmp/`**. The reason is that `/tmp` in stage1 is in the RAM disk and will get lost after the reboot, but the installed system is already mounted at `/mnt/`. `<file>/tmp/answer_hostname</file>`	This information is optional, but you should at least provide `path` or `file`.
`password`	If this boolean is set to `true`, a password dialog pops up instead of a simple text entry. Setting this to `true` only makes sense if `type` is string.	Optional. The default is `false`.

Element	Description	Comment
	`<password config:type="boolean">true</password>`	
stage	Stage configures the installation stage in which the question pops up. You can set this value to `cont` or `initial`. `initial` means the pop-up comes up very early in the installation, shortly after the pre-script has run. `cont` means, that the dialog with the question comes after the first reboot when the system boots for the very first time. Questions you answer during the `inital` stage will write their answer into the control file on the hard disk. You should know that if you enter clear text passwords during `initial`. Of course it does not make sense to ask for the file system to use during the `cont` phase. The hard disk is already partitioned at that stage and the question will have no effect. `<stage>cont</stage>`	Optional. The default is `initial`.

Element	Description	Comment
`selection`	The selection element contains a list of `entry` elements. Each entry represents a possible option for the user to choose. The user cannot enter a value in a text box, but he can choose from a list of values. <selection config:type="list"> <entry> <value> btrfs </value> <label> Btrfs File System </label> </entry> <entry> <value> ext3 </value> <label> Extended3 File System </label> </entry> </selection>	Optional for `type=string`, not possible for `type=boolean` and mandatory for `type=symbol`.
`dialog`	You can ask more than one question per dialog. To do so, specify the dialog-id with an integer. All questions with	Optional.

Element	Description	Comment
	the same dialog-id belong to the same dialog. The dialogs are sorted by the id too. `<dialog config:type="integer">3</dialog>`	
`element`	you can have more than one question per dialog. To make that possible you need to specify the element-id with an integer. The questions in a dialog are sorted by id. `<element config:type="integer">1</element>`	Optional (see dialog).
`width`	You can increase the default width of dialog. If there are multiple width specifications per dialog, the largest one is used. The number is roughly equivalent to the number of characters. `<width config:type="integer">50</width>`	Optional.
`height`	You can increase default height of dialog. If there are multiple height specifications per dialog, largest one is	Optional.

Element	Description	Comment
	used. The number is roughly equivalent to number of lines. `<height config:type="integer">15</height>`	
`frametitle`	You can have more than one question per dialog. Each question on a dialog has a frame that can have a frame title, a small caption for each question. You can put multiple elements into one frame. They need to have the same frame title. `<frametitle>User data</frametitle>`	Optional. Default is no frame title.
`script`	You can run scripts after a question has been answered (see the table below for detailed instructions about scripts). `<script>...</script>`	Optional (default is no script).
`ok_label`	You can change the label on the *Ok* button. The last element that specifies the label for a dialog wins.	Optional.

Element	Description	Comment
	`<ok_label>Finish</ok_label>`	
`back_label`	You can change the label on the *Back* button. The last element that specifies the label for a dialog wins. `<back_label>change values</back_label>`	Optional.
`timeout`	You can specify an integer here that is used as timeout in seconds. If the user does not answer the question before the timeout, the default value is taken as answer. When the user touches or changes any widget in the dialog, the timeout is turned off and the dialog needs to be confirmed via the ok-button. `<timeout config:type="integer">30</timeout>`	Optional. A missing value is interpreted as `0`, which means that there is no timeout.
`default_value_script`	You can run scripts to set the default value for a question (see Section 4.33.1, "Default Value Scripts" for detailed instructions about default value scripts). This feature is	Optional. Default is no script.

Element	Description	Comment
	useful if you can calculate a default value, especially in combination with the timeout option. `<default_value_script>...</default_value_script>`	

4.33.1 Default Value Scripts

You can run scripts to set the default value for a question. This feature is useful if you can calculate a default value, especially in combination with the timeout option.

The elements listed below must be placed within the following XML structure:

```
<general>
  <ask-list config:type="list">
    <ask>
      <default_value_script>
        ...
      </default_value_script>
    </ask>
  </ask-list>
</general>
```

TABLE 4.5: DEFAULT VALUE SCRIPTS: XML REPRESENTATION

Element	Description	Comment
source	The source code of the script. Whatever you **echo** to STDOUT will be used as default value for the ask-dialog. If your script has an exit code other than 0, the normal default element is used. Take	This value is required, otherwise nothing would be executed.

Element	Description	Comment
	care you use **echo -n** to suppress the \n and that you echo reasonable values and not “okay” for a boolean `<source>...</source>`	
interpreter	The interpreter to use. `<interpreter>perl</interpreter>`	The default value is shell. You can also set /bin/myinterpreter as value.

4.33.2 Scripts

You can run scripts after a question has been answered.

The elements listed below must be placed within the following XML structure:

```
<general>
  <ask-list config:type="list">
    <ask>
      <script>
        ...
      </script>
    </ask>
  </ask-list>
</general>
```

TABLE 4.6: SCRIPTS: XML REPRESENTATION

Element	Description	Comment
file name	The file name of the script. `<filename>my_ask_script.sh</filename>`	The default is ask_script.sh

Element	Description	Comment
`source`	The source code of the script. Together with `rerun_on_error` activated, you check the value that was entered for sanity. Your script can create a file `/tmp/next_dialog` with a dialog id specifying the next dialog AutoYaST will raise. A value of -1 terminates the ask sequence. If that file is not created, AutoYaST will run the dialogs in the normal order (since 11.0 only). `<source>...</source>`	This value is required, otherwise nothing would be executed.
`environment`	A boolean that passes the value of the answer to the question as an environment variable to the script. The variable is named `VAL`. `<environment config:type="boolean">true</environment>`	Optional. Default is `false`.
`feedback`	A boolean that turns on feedback for the script execution. STDOUT will be displayed in a pop-up window that must be confirmed after the script execution.	Optional, default is `false`.

Element	Description	Comment
	`<feedback config:type="boolean">true</feedback>`	
`debug`	A boolean that turns on debugging for the script execution. `<debug config:type="boolean">true</debug>`	Optional, default is `true`. This value needs `feedback` to be turned on, too.
`rerun_on_error`	A boolean that keeps the dialog open until the script has an exit code of 0 (zero). So you can parse and check the answers the user gave in the script and display an error with the `feedback` option. `<rerun_on_error config:type="boolean">true</rerun_on_error>`	Optional, default is `false`. This value should be used together with the feedback option.

Below you can see an example of the usage of the `ask` feature.

```
<general>
  <ask-list config:type="list">
    <ask>
      <pathlist config:type="list">
        <path>ldap,ldap_server</path>
      </pathlist>
      <stage>cont</stage>
      <help>Choose your server depending on your department</help>
      <selection config:type="list">
```

```
        <entry>
          <value>ldap1.mydom.de</value>
          <label>LDAP for development</label>
        </entry>
        <entry>
          <value>ldap2.mydom.de</value>
          <label>LDAP for sales</label>
        </entry>
      </selection>
      <default>ldap2.mydom.de</default>
      <default_value_script>
        <source> <![CDATA[
echo -n "ldap1.mydom.de"
]]>
        </source>
      </default_value_script>
    </ask>
    <ask>
      <pathlist config:type="list">
        <path>networking,dns,hostname</path>
      </pathlist>
      <question>Enter Hostname</question>
      <stage>initial</stage>
      <default>enter your hostname here</default>
    </ask>
    <ask>
      <pathlist config:type="list">
        <path>partitioning,0,partitions,0,filesystem</path>
      </pathlist>
      <question>File System</question>
      <type>symbol</type>
      <selection config:type="list">
        <entry>
          <value config:type="symbol">reiser</value>
          <label>default File System (recommended)</label>
        </entry>
```

```
        <entry>
          <value config:type="symbol">ext3</value>
          <label>Fallback File System</label>
        </entry>
      </selection>
    </ask>
  </ask-list>
</general>
```

The following example shows a to choose between AutoYaST control files. AutoYaST will read the `modified.xml` file again after the ask-dialogs are done. This way you can fetch a complete new control file.

```
<general>
  <ask-list config:type="list">
    <ask>
      <selection config:type="list">
        <entry>
          <value>part1.xml</value>
          <label>Simple partitioning</label>
        </entry>
        <entry>
          <value>part2.xml</value>
          <label>encrypted /tmp</label>
        </entry>
        <entry>
          <value>part3.xml</value>
          <label>LVM</label>
        </entry>
      </selection>
      <title>XML Profile</title>
      <question>Choose a profile</question>
      <stage>initial</stage>
      <default>part1.xml</default>
      <script>
        <filename>fetch.sh</filename>
```

```
        <environment config:type="boolean">true</environment>
        <source>
<![CDATA[
wget http://10.10.0.162/$VAL -O /tmp/profile/modified.xml 2>/dev/null
]]>
        </source>
        <debug config:type="boolean">false</debug>
        <feedback config:type="boolean">false</feedback>
      </script>
    </ask>tion>
  </ask-list>
</general>
```

You can verify the answer of a question with a script like this:

```
<general>
  <ask-list config:type="list">
    <ask>
      <script>
        <filename>my.sh</filename>
        <rerun_on_error config:type="boolean">true</rerun_on_error>
        <environment config:type="boolean">true</environment>
        <source><![CDATA[
if [ "$VAL" = "myhost" ]; then
    echo "Illegal Hostname!";
    exit 1;
fi
exit 0
]]>
        </source>
        <debug config:type="boolean">false</debug>
        <feedback config:type="boolean">true</feedback>
      </script>
      <dialog config:type="integer">0</dialog>
      <element config:type="integer">0</element>
      <pathlist config:type="list">
```

```
        <path>networking,dns,hostname</path>
      </pathlist>
      <question>Enter Hostname</question>
      <default>enter your hostname here</default>
    </ask>
  </ask-list>
</general>
```

4.34 Kernel Dumps

Note: Availability

This feature is not available on the IBM System z (s390x) architecture.

With Kdump the system can create crashdump files if the whole kernel crashes. Crash dump files contain the memory contents while the system crashed. Such core files can be analyzed later by support or a (kernel) developer to find the reason for the system crash. Kdump is mostly useful for servers where you cannot easily reproduce such crashes but it is important to get the problem fixed.

The only downside: enabling Kdump costs you between 64 MB and 128 MB of system RAM (on “normal” sized systems), reserved for Kdump in case the system crashes and the dump needs to be generated.

This section only describes how to set up Kdump with AutoYaST. It does not describe how Kdump works. For details, refer to the kdump(7) manual page.

The following example shows a general Kdump configuration.

EXAMPLE 4.48: KDUMP CONFIGURATION

```
<kdump>
  <!-- memory reservation -->
  <add_crash_kernel config:type="boolean">true</add_crash_kernel>
  <crash_kernel>256M-:64M</crash_kernel>
  <general>
```

```
    <!-- dump target settings -->
    <KDUMP_SAVEDIR>ftp://stravinsky.suse.de/incoming/dumps</KDUMP_SAVEDIR>
    <KDUMP_COPY_KERNEL>true</KDUMP_COPY_KERNEL>
    <KDUMP_FREE_DISK_SIZE>64</KDUMP_FREE_DISK_SIZE>
    <KDUMP_KEEP_OLD_DUMPS>5</KDUMP_KEEP_OLD_DUMPS>

    <!-- filtering and compression -->
    <KDUMP_DUMPFORMAT>compressed</KDUMP_DUMPFORMAT>
    <KDUMP_DUMPLEVEL>1</KDUMP_DUMPLEVEL>

    <!-- notification -->
    <KDUMP_NOTIFICATION_TO>tux@example.com</KDUMP_NOTIFICATION_TO>
    <KDUMP_NOTIFICATION_CC>spam@example.com devnull@example.com</
KDUMP_NOTIFICATION_CC>
    <KDUMP_SMTP_SERVER>mail.example.com</KDUMP_SMTP_SERVER>
    <KDUMP_SMTP_USER></KDUMP_SMTP_USER>
    <KDUMP_SMTP_PASSWORD></KDUMP_SMTP_PASSWORD>

    <!-- kdump kernel -->
    <KDUMP_KERNELVER></KDUMP_KERNELVER>
    <KDUMP_COMMANDLINE></KDUMP_COMMANDLINE>
    <KDUMP_COMMANDLINE_APPEND></KDUMP_COMMANDLINE_APPEND>

    <!-- expert settings -->
    <KDUMP_IMMEDIATE_REBOOT>yes</KDUMP_IMMEDIATE_REBOOT>
    <KDUMP_VERBOSE>15</KDUMP_VERBOSE>
    <KEXEC_OPTIONS></KEXEC_OPTIONS>
  </general>
</kdump>
```

4.34.1 Memory Reservation

The first step is to reserve memory for Kdump at boot-up. Because the memory must be reserved very early during the boot process, the configuration is done via a kernel command line parameter called `crashkernel`. The reserved memory will be used to load a second kernel which will be executed without rebooting if the first kernel crashes. This second kernel has a special initrd, which contains all programs necessary to save the dump over the network or to disk, send a notification e-mail, and finally reboot.

To reserve memory for Kdump, specify the `amount` (such as `64M` to reserve 64 MB of memory from the RAM) and the `offset`. The syntax is `crashkernel=AMOUNT@OFFSET`. The kernel can auto-detect the right offset (except for the Xen hypervisor, where you need to specify `16M` as offset). The amount of memory that needs to be reserved depends on architecture and main memory—refer to *Book* "System Analysis and Tuning Guide", *Chapter 17 "Kexec and Kdump", Section 17.7.1 "Manual Kdump Configuration"* for recommendations on the amount of memory to reserve for Kdump.

You can also use the extended command line syntax to specify the amount of reserved memory depending on the System RAM. That is useful if you share one AutoYaST control file for multiple installations or if you often remove or install memory on one machine. The syntax is:

```
BEGIN_RANGE_1-END_RANGE_1:AMOUNT_1,BEGIN_RANGE_2-END_RANGE_2:AMOUNT_2@OFFSET
```

`BEGIN_RANGE_1` is the start of the first memory range (for example: `0M`) and `END_RANGE_1` is the end of the first memory range (can be empty in case `infinity` should be assumed) and so on. For example `256M-2G:64M,2G-:128M` means to reserve 64 MB of crashkernel memory if the system has between 256 MB and 2 GB RAM and to reserve 128 MB of crashkernel memory if the system has more than 2 GB RAM.

On the other hand, it is possible to specify multiple values for crashkernel parameter, for example, when wanting to reserve different segments of low and high memory. In this case use values like `72M,low` and `256M,high`:

EXAMPLE 4.49: KDUMP MEMORY RESERVATION WITH MULTIPLE VALUES

```
<kdump>
  <!-- memory reservation (high and low) -->
  <add_crash_kernel config:type="boolean">true</add_crash_kernel>
  <crash_kernel>
    <listentry>72M,low</listentry>
    <listentry>256M,high</listentry>
  </crash_kernel>
</kdump>
```

The following table shows the settings necessary to reserve memory:

TABLE 4.7: KDUMP MEMORY RESERVATION SETTINGS:XML REPRESENTATION

Element	Description	Comment
`add_crash_Kernel`	Set to `true` if memory should be reserved and Kdump enabled. `<add_crash_kernel config:type="boolean">true</add_crash_kernel>`	required

`crash_Kernel`	Use the syntax of the crashkernel command line as discussed above.
	`<crash_kernel>256M:64M</crash_kernel>`
	A list of values is also supported.
	`<crash_kernel>`
	`  <listentry>72M,low</listentry>`
	`  <listentry>256M,high</listentry>`
	`</crash_kernel>`
		required

4.34.2 Dump Saving

4.34.2.1 Target

The element `KDUMP_SAVEDIR` specifies the URL to where the dump is saved. The following methods are possible:

- `file` to save to the local disk,
- `ftp` to save to an FTP server (without encryption),
- `sftp` to save to an SSH2 SFTP server,
- `nfs` to save to an NFS location and
- `cifs` to save the dump to a CIFS/SMP export from Samba or Microsoft Windows.

For details see the kdump(5) manual page. Two examples are: `file:///var/crash` (which is the default location according to FHS) and `ftp://user:password@host:port/incoming/dumps`. A subdirectory, with the time stamp contained in the name, will be created and the dumps saved there.

When the dump is saved to the local disk, `KDUMP_KEEP_OLD_DUMPS` can be used to delete old dumps automatically. Set it to the number of old dumps that should be kept. If the target partition would end up with less free disk space than specified in `KDUMP_FREE_DISK_SIZE`, the dump is not saved.

If you want to save the whole kernel and the debug information (if installed) to the same directory, set `KDUMP_COPY_KERNEL` to `true`. You will have everything you need to analyze the dump in one directory (except kernel modules and their debugging information).

4.34.2.2 Filtering and Compression

The kernel dump is uncompressed and unfiltered. It can get as large as your system RAM. To get smaller files, compress the dump file afterwards. The dump needs to be decompressed before opening.

To use page compression, which compresses every page and allows dynamic decompression with the crash(8) debugging tool, set `KDUMP_DUMPFORMAT` to `compressed` (default).

You may not want to save all memory pages, for example those filled with zeroes. To filter the dump, set the `KDUMP_DUMPLEVEL`. 0 produces a full dump and 31 is the smallest dump. The manual pages kdump(5) and makedumpfile(8) list for each value which pages will be saved.

4.34.2.3 Summary

TABLE 4.8: DUMP TARGET SETTINGS: XML REPRESENTATION

Element	Description	Comment
KDUMP_SAVEDIR	A URL that specifies the target to which the dump and related files will be saved. `<KDUMP_SAVEDIR>file:///var/crash/</KDUMP_SAVEDIR>`	required
KDUMP_COPY_KERNEL	Set to `true`, if not only the dump should be saved to `KDUMP_SAVEDIR` but also the kernel and its debugging information (if installed). `<KDUMP_COPY_KERNEL>false</KDUMP_COPY_KERNEL>`	optional
KDUMP_FREE_DISK_SIZE	Disk space in megabytes that must remain free after saving the dump. If not enough space is available, the dump will not be saved. `<KDUMP_FREE_DISK_SIZE>64</KDUMP_FREE_DISK_SIZE>`	optional
KDUMP_KEEP_OLD_DUMPS	The number of dumps that are kept (not deleted) if `KDUMP_SAVEDIR` points to a local directory. Specify 0 if you do not want any dumps to be automatically deleted,	optional

Element	Description	Comment
	specify -1 if all dumps except the current one should be deleted. `<KDUMP_KEEP_OLD_DUMPS>4</KDUMP_KEEP_OLD_DUMPS>`	

4.34.3 E-Mail Notification

Configure e-mail notification if you want to be informed when a machine crashes and a dump is saved.

Because Kdump runs in the initrd, a local mail server cannot send the notification e-mail. An SMTP server needs to be specified (see below).

You need to provide exactly one address in `KDUMP_NOTIFICATION_TO`. More addresses can be specified in `KDUMP_NOTIFICATION_CC`. Only use e-mail addresses in both cases, not a real name.

Specify `KDUMP_SMTP_SERVER` and (if the server needs authentication) `KDUMP_SMTP_USER` and `KDUMP_SMTP_PASSWORD`. Support for TSL or SSL is not available but may be added in the future.

TABLE 4.9: E-MAIL NOTIFICATION SETTINGS: XML REPRESENTATION

Element	Description	Comment
`KDUMP_NOTIFICATION_TO`	Exactly one e-mail address to which the e-mail should be sent. Additional recipients can be specified in `KDUMP_NOTIFICATION_CC`. `<KDUMP_NOTIFICATION_TO>tux@example.com</KDUMP_NOTIFICATION_TO>`	optional (notification disabled if empty)
`KDUMP_NOTIFICATION_CC`	Zero, one or more recipients that are in the cc line of the notification e-mail.	optional

Element	Description	Comment
	`<KDUMP_NOTIFICATION_CC >wilber@example.com geeko@example.com</ KDUMP_NOTIFICATION_CC>`	
`KDUMP_SMTP_SERVER`	Host name of the SMTP server used for mail delivery. SMTP authentication is supported (see `KDUMP_SMTP_USER` and `KDUMP_SMTP_PASSWORD`) but TSL and SSL are not>. `<KDUMP_SMTP_SERVER>email.suse.de</ KDUMP_SMTP_SERVER>`	optional (notification disabled if empty)
`KDUMP_SMTP_USER`	User name used together with `KDUMP_SMTP_PASSWORD` for SMTP authentication. `<KDUMP_SMTP_USER>bwalle</ KDUMP_SMTP_USER>`	optional
`KDUMP_SMTP_PASSWORD`	Password used together with `KDUMP_SMTP_USER` for SMTP authentication. `<KDUMP_SMTP_PASSWORD>geheim</ KDUMP_SMTP_PASSWORD>`	optional

4.34.4 Kdump Kernel Settings

As already mentioned, a special kernel is booted to save the dump. If you do not want to use the auto-detection mechanism to find out which kernel is used (see the kdump(5) manual page that describes the algorithm which is used to find the kernel), you can specify the version of a custom kernel in `KDUMP_KERNELVER`. If you set it to `foo`, then the kernel located in `/boot/vmlinuz-foo` or `/boot/vmlinux-foo` (in that order on platforms that have a `vmlinuz` file) will be used.

You can specify the command line used to boot the Kdump kernel. Normally the boot command line is used minus some settings that make no sense with Kdump (like the `crashkernel` parameter) plus some settings needed by Kdump (see the manual page kdump(5)). If you want some additional parameters like an overwritten console setting then use `KDUMP_COMMANDLINE_APPEND`. If you know what you are doing and you want to specify the whole command line, set `KDUMP_COMMANDLINE`.

TABLE 4.10: KERNEL SETTINGS: XML REPRESENTATION

Element	Description	Comment
`KDUMP_KERNELVER`	Version string for the kernel used for Kdump. Leave it empty to use the auto-detection mechanism (strongly recommended). `<KDUMP_KERNELVER >2.6.27-default</ KDUMP_KERNELVER>`	optional (auto-detection if empty)
`KDUMP_COMMANDLINE_APPEND`	Additional command line parameters for the Kdump kernel. `<KDUMP_COMMANDLINE_APPEND >console=ttyS0,57600</ KDUMP_COMMANDLINE_APPEND>`	optional

<table>
<tr><th>Element</th><th>Description</th><th>Comment</th></tr>
<tr><td><code>KDUMP_Command Line</code></td><td>Overwrite the automatically generated Kdump command line. Use with care. Usually, <code>KDUMP_COMMANDLINE_APPEND</code> should suffice.

<code><KDUMP_COMMANDLINE_APPEND
>root=/dev/sda5
 maxcpus=1 irqpoll</
KDUMP_COMMANDLINE></code></td><td>optional</td></tr>
</table>

4.34.5 Expert Settings

TABLE 4.11: EXPERT SETTINGS: XML REPRESENTATIONS

<table>
<tr><th>Element</th><th>Description</th><th>Comment</th></tr>
<tr><td><code>KDUMP_IMMEDIATE_REBOOT</code></td><td><code>true</code> if the system should be rebooted automatically after the dump has been saved, <code>false</code> otherwise. The default is to reboot the system automatically.

<code><KDUMP_IMMEDIATE_REBOOT
>true</
KDUMP_IMMEDIATE_REBOOT></code></td><td>optional</td></tr>
<tr><td><code>KDUMP_VERBOSE</code></td><td>Bitmask that specifies how verbose the Kdump process should be. Read kdump(5) for details.</td><td>optional</td></tr>
</table>

Element	Description	Comment
	`<KDUMP_VERBOSE>3</ KDUMP_VERBOSE>`	
`KEXEC_OPTIONS`	Additional options that are passed to kexec when loading the Kdump kernel. Normally empty. `<KEXEC_OPTIONS>--noio</ KEXEC_OPTIONS>`	optional

4.35 Miscellaneous Hardware and System Components

In addition to the core component configuration, like network authentication and security, AutoYaST offers a wide range of hardware and system configuration options, the same as available by default on any system installed manually and in an interactive way. For example, it is possible to configure printers, sound devices, TV cards and any other hardware components which have a module within YaST.

Any new configuration options added to YaST will be automatically available in AutoYaST.

4.35.1 Printer

AutoYaST support for printing is limited to basic settings defining how CUPS is used on a client for printing via the network.

There is no AutoYaST support for setting up local print queues. Modern printers are usually connected via USB. CUPS accesses USB printers by a model-specific device URI like `usb://ACME/FunPrinter?serial=1a2b3c`. Usually it is not possible to predict the correct USB device URI in advance, because it is determined by the CUPS back-end `usb` during runtime. Therefore it is not possible to set up local print queues with AutoYaST.

Basics on how CUPS is used on a client workstation to print via network:

On client workstations application programs submit print jobs to the CUPS daemon process (`cupsd`). `cupsd` forwards the print jobs to a CUPS print server in the network where the print jobs are processed. The server sends the printer specific data to the printer device.

If there is only a single CUPS print server in the network, there is no need to have a CUPS daemon running on each client workstation. Instead it is simpler to specify the CUPS server in `/etc/cups/client.conf` and access it directly (only one CUPS server entry can be set). In this case application programs that run on client workstations submit print jobs directly to the specified CUPS print server.

Example 4.50, "Printer configuration" shows a `printer` configuration section. The `cupsd_conf_content` entry contains the whole verbatim content of the `cupsd` configuration file `/etc/cups/cupsd.conf`. The `client_conf_content` entry contains the whole verbatim content of `/etc/cups/client.conf`. The `printer` section contains the `cupsd` configuration but it does not specify whether the cupsd should run.

EXAMPLE 4.50: PRINTER CONFIGURATION

```
  <printer>
    <client_conf_content>
      <file_contents><![CDATA[
... verbatim content of /etc/cups/client.conf ...
]]></file_contents>
    </client_conf_content>
    <cupsd_conf_content>
      <file_contents><![CDATA[
... verbatim content of /etc/cups/cupsd.conf ...
]]></file_contents>
    </cupsd_conf_content>
  </printer>
```

Note: `/etc/cups/cups-files.conf`

With release 1.6 the CUPS configuration file has been split into two files: `cupsd.conf` and `cups-files.conf`. As of SUSE Linux Enterprise Server 12, AutoYaST only supports modifying `cupsd.conf` since the default settings in `cups-files.conf` are sufficient for usual printing setups.

4.35.2 Sound devices

An example of the sound configuration created using the configuration system is shown below.

EXAMPLE 4.51: SOUND CONFIGURATION

```
<sound>
  <autoinstall config:type="boolean">true</autoinstall>
  <modules_conf config:type="list">
    <module_conf>
      <alias>snd-card-0</alias>
      <model>M5451, ALI</model>
      <module>snd-ali5451</module>
      <options>
        <snd_enable>1</snd_enable>
        <snd_index>0</snd_index>
        <snd_pcm_channels>32</snd_pcm_channels>
      </options>
    </module_conf>
  </modules_conf>
  <volume_settings config:type="list">
    <listentry>
      <Master config:type="integer">75</Master>
    </listentry>
  </volume_settings>
</sound>
```

5 Rules and Classes

5.1 Rules-based Automatic Installation

Rules offer the possibility to configure a system depending on system attributes by merging multiple control files during installation. The rules-based installation is controlled by a rules file. This is useful to install, for example, systems in two departments in one go. Assume a scenario where machines in department A need to be installed as office desktops, whereas machines in department B need to be installed as developer workstations. You would create a rules file with two different rules. For each rule, you could use different system parameters to distinguish the installations from one another. Each rule would also contain a link to an appropriate profile for each department.

The rules file is an XML file containing rules for each group of systems (or single systems) that you want to automatically install. A set of rules distinguish a group of systems based on one or more system attributes. After passing all rules, each group of systems is linked to a control file. Both the rules file and the control files must be located in a pre-defined and accessible location.

The rules file is retrieved only if no specific control file is supplied using the `autoyast` keyword. For example, if the following is used, the rules file will not be evaluated:

```
autoyast=http://10.10.0.1/profile/myprofile.xml
autoyast=http://10.10.0.1/profile/rules/rules.xml
```

Instead use:

```
autoyast=http://10.10.0.1/profile/
```

which will load `http://10.10.0.1/profile/rules/rules.xml` (the slash at the end of the directory name is important).

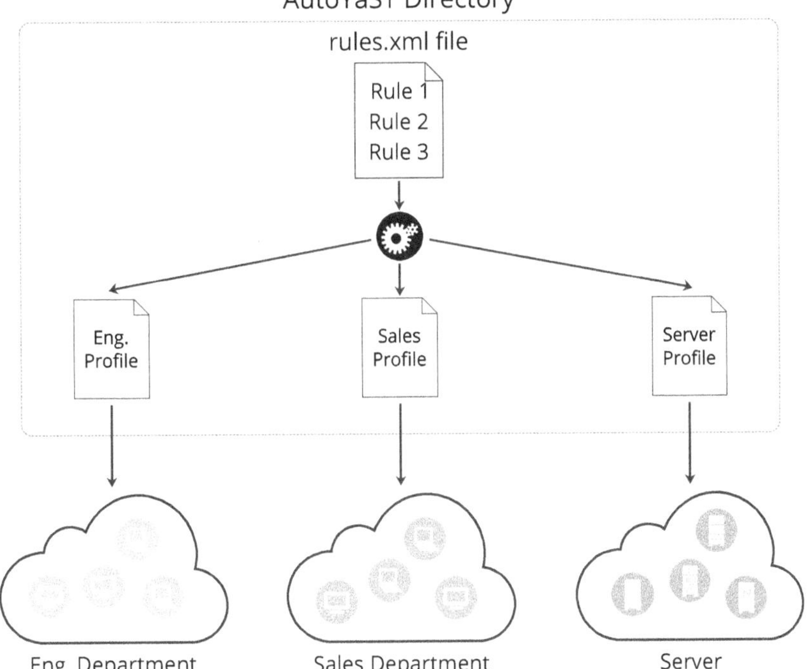

FIGURE 5.1: RULES

If more than one rule applies, the final control file for each group is generated on the fly using a merge script. The merging process is based on the order of the rules and later rules override configuration data in earlier rules. Note that the names of the top sections in the merged xml files need to be in alphabetical order for the merge to succeed.

The use of a rules file is optional. If the rules file is not found, system installation proceeds in the classic way by only using the supplied control file or by searching for the control file depending on the MAC or the IP address of the system.

5.1.1 Rules File Explained

EXAMPLE 5.1: SIMPLE RULES FILE

The following simple example illustrates how the rules file is used to retrieve the configuration for a client with known hardware.

```
<?xml version="1.0"?>
<!DOCTYPE autoinstall>
```

```
<autoinstall xmlns="http://www.suse.com/1.0/yast2ns" xmlns:config="http://
www.suse.com/1.0/configns">
  <rules config:type="list">
    <rule>
       <disksize>
            <match>/dev/sdc 1000</match>
            <match_type>greater</match_type>
       </disksize>
       <result>
            <profile>department_a.xml</profile>
            <continue config:type="boolean">false</continue>
        </result>
    </rule>
    <rule>
       <disksize>
            <match>/dev/sda 1000</match>
            <match_type>greater</match_type>
       </disksize>
       <result>
            <profile>department_b.xml</profile>
            <continue config:type="boolean">false</continue>
        </result>
    </rule>
  </rules>
</autoinstall>
```

The last example defines two rules and provides a different control file for every rule. The rule used in this case is `disksize`. After parsing the rules file, YaST attempts to match the target system with the rules in the `rules.xml` file. A rule match occurs when the target system matches all system attributes defined in the rule. As soon as the system matches a rule, the respective resource is added to the stack of control files AutoYaST will use to create the final control file. The `continue` property tells AutoYaST whether it should continue with other rules after a match has been found.

If the first rule does not match, the next rule in the list is examined until a match is found.

Using the `disksize` attribute, you can provide different configurations for systems with hard disks of different sizes. The first rule checks if the device `/dev/sdc` is available and if it is greater than 1 GB in size using the `match` property.

A rule must have at least one attribute to be matched. If you need to check more attributes, such as memory or architectures, you can add more attributes in the rule resource as shown in the next example.

EXAMPLE 5.2: SIMPLE RULES FILE

The following example illustrates how the rules file is used to retrieve the configuration for a client with known hardware.

```
<?xml version="1.0"?>
<!DOCTYPE autoinstall>
<autoinstall xmlns="http://www.suse.com/1.0/yast2ns" xmlns:config="http://
www.suse.com/1.0/configns">
  <rules config:type="list">
    <rule>
      <disksize>
           <match>/dev/sdc 1000</match>
           <match_type>greater</match_type>
      </disksize>
      <memsize>
           <match>1000</match>
           <match_type>greater</match_type>
      </memsize>
      <result>
           <profile>department_a.xml</profile>
           <continue config:type="boolean">false</continue>
       </result>
    </rule>
    <rule>
      <disksize>
           <match>/dev/shda 1000</match>
           <match_type>greater</match_type>
      </disksize>
      <memsize>
```

```
          <match>256</match>
          <match_type>greater</match_type>
      </memsize>
      <result>
          <profile>department_b.xml</profile>
          <continue config:type="boolean">false</continue>
       </result>
    </rule>
  </rules>
</autoinstall>
```

The rules directory must be located in the same directory specified via the `autoyast` keyword at boot time. If the client was booted using `autoyast=http://10.10.0.1/profiles/`, AutoYaST will search for the rules file at http://10.10.0.1/profiles/rules/rules.xml.

5.1.2 Custom Rules

If the attributes AutoYaST provides for rules are not enough for your purposes, use custom rules. Custom rules contain a shell script. The output of the script (STDOUT, STDERR is ignored) can be evaluated.

Here is an example for the use of custom rules:

```
<rule>
  <custom1>
    <script>
if grep -i intel /proc/cpuinfo > /dev/null; then
echo -n "intel"
else
echo -n "non_intel"
fi;
    </script>
    <match>*</match>
    <match_type>exact</match_type>
  </custom1>
  <result>
```

```
    <profile>@custom1@.xml</profile>
    <continue config:type="boolean">true</continue>
  </result>
</rule>
```

The script in this rule can echo either `intel` or `non_intel` to STDOUT (the output of the grep command must be directed to /dev/null in this case). The output of the rule script will be filled between the two '@' characters, to determine the file name of the control file to fetch. AutoYaST will read the output and fetch a file with the name `intel.xml` or `non_intel.xml`. This file can contain the AutoYaST profile part for the software selection, for example, in case you want a different software selection on intel hardware than on others.

The number of custom rules is limited to five. So you can use `custom1` to `custom5`.

5.1.3 Match Types for Rules

You can use five different match_types:

- `exact` (default)
- `greater`
- `lower`
- `range`
- `regex` (a simple `=~` operator like in Bash)

If using `exact`, the string must match exactly as specified. `regex` can be used to match substrings like `ntel` will match Intel, intel and intelligent. `greater` and `lower` can be used for `memsize` or `totaldisk` for example. They can match only with rules that return an integer value. A range is only possible for integer values too and has the form of `value1-value2`, for example `512-1024`.

5.1.4 Combine Attributes

Multiple attributes can be combined via a logical operator. It is possible to let a rule match if `disksize` is greater than 1GB or `memsize` is exactly 512MB.

You can do this with the `operator` element in the rules.xml file. `and` and `or` are possible operators, `and` being the default. Here is an example:

```
<rule>
  <disksize>
    <match>/dev/sda 1000</match>
    <match_type>greater</match_type>
  </disksize>
  <memsize>
    <match>256</match>
    <match_type>greater</match_type>
  </memsize>
  <result>
    <profile>machine2.xml</profile>
    <continue config:type="boolean">false</continue>
  </result>
  <operator>or</operator>
</rule>
```

5.1.5 Rules File Structure

The `rules.xml` file needs to:

- have at least one rule,
- have the name `rules.xml`,
- be located in the directory `rules` in the profile repository,
- have at least one attribute to match in the rule.

5.1.6 Predefined System Attributes

The following table lists the predefined system attributes you can match in the rules file.

If you are unsure about a value on your system, run `/usr/lib/YaST/bin/y2base ayast_probe ncurses`. The text box displaying the detected values can be scrolled. Note that this command will not work while another YaST process that requires a lock (for example the installer) is running. Therefore you cannot run it during the installation.

TABLE 5.1: SYSTEM ATTRIBUTES

Attribute	**Values**	**Description**
`hostaddress`	IP address of the host	This attribute must always match exactly.
`host name`	The name of the host	This attribute must always match exactly.
`domain`	Domain name of host	This attribute must always match exactly.
`installed_product`	The name of the product to be installed.	This attribute must always match exactly.
`installed_product_version`	The version of the product to be installed.	This attribute must always match exactly.
`network`	network address of host	This attribute must always match exactly.
`mac`	MAC address of host	This attribute must always match exactly (the MAC addresses should have the form `0080c8f6484c`).
`linux`	Number of installed Linux partitions on the system	This attribute can be 0 or more.
`others`	Number of installed non-Linux partitions on the system	This attribute can be 0 or more.
`xserver`	X Server needed for graphic adapter	This attribute must always match exactly.

Attribute	Values	Description
`memsize`	Memory available on host in MBytes	All match types are available.
`totaldisk`	Total disk space available on host in MBytes	All match types are available.
`haspcmcia`	System has PCMCIA (i.e Laptops)	Exact match required, `1` for having PCMCIA or `0` for not having it.
`hostid`	Hex representation of the IP address	Exact match required
`arch`	Architecture of host	Exact match required
`karch`	Kernel Architecture of host (for example SMP kernel, Xen Kernel)	Exact match required
`disksize`	Drive device and size	All match types are available.
`product`	The hardware product name as specified in SMBIOS	Exact match required
`product_vendor`	The hardware vendor as specified in SMBIOS	Exact match required
`board`	The system board name as specified in SMBIOS	Exact match required
`board_vendor`	The system board vendor as specified in SMBIOS	Exact match required
`custom1-5`	Custom rules using shell scripts	All match types are available.

5.1.7 Rules with Dialogs

You can use dialog pop-ups with check boxes to select rules you want matched.

The elements listed below must be placed within the following XML structure in the `rules.xml` file:

```
<rules config:type="list">
  <rule>
    <dialog>
      ...
    </dialog>
  </rule>
</rules>
```

Attribute	Values	Description
`dialog_nr`	All rules with the same `dialog_nr` are presented in the same pop-up dialog. The same `dialog_nr` can appear in multiple rules. `<dialog_nr config:type="integer">3</dialog_nr>`	This element is optional and the default for a missing dialog_nr is always `0`. If you want to use one pop-up for all rules, you do not need to specify the `dialog_nr`.
`element`	Specify a unique ID. Even if you have more than one dialog, you must not use the same id twice. Using id `1` on dialog 1 and id `1` on dialog 2 is not supported. (This behavior is contrary to the `ask` dialog, where you can have the same ID for multiple dialogs.)	Optional. If left out, AutoYaST adds its own ids internally. Then you cannot specify conflicting rules (see below).

Attribute	Values	Description
	`<element config:type="integer">3</element>`	
`title`	Caption of the pop-up dialog `<title>Desktop Selection</title>`	Optional
`question`	Question shown in the pop-up behind the check box. `<question>GNOME Desktop</question>`	Optional. If you do not configure a text here, the name of the XML file that is triggered by this rule will be shown instead.
`timeout`	Timeout in seconds after which the dialog will automatically "press" the okay button. Useful for a non-blocking installation in combination with rules dialogs. `<timeout config:type="integer">30</timeout>`	Optional. A missing timeout will stop the installation process until the dialog is confirmed by the user.
`conflicts`	A list of element ids (rules) that conflict with this rule. If this rule matches or is selected by the user, all conflicting rules are deselected and disabled in the pop-up. Take care that you do not create deadlocks.	`optional`

Attribute	Values	Description
	`<conflicts config:type="list"> <element config:type="integer">1</element> <element config:type="integer">5</element> ... </conflicts>`	

Here is an example of how to use dialogs with rules:

```
<rules config:type="list">
  <rule>
    <custom1>
      <script>
echo -n 100
      </script>
      <match>100</match>
      <match_type>exact</match_type>
    </custom1>
    <result>
      <profile>rules/gnome.xml</profile>
      <continue config:type="boolean">true</continue>
    </result>
    <dialog>
      <element config:type="integer">0</element>
      <question>GNOME Desktop</question>
      <title>Desktop Selection</title>
      <conflicts config:type="list">
        <element config:type="integer">1</element>
      </conflicts>
      <dialog_nr config:type="integer">0</dialog_nr>
```

```
    </dialog>
  </rule>
  <rule>
    <custom1>
      <script>
echo -n 100
      </script>
      <match>101</match>
      <match_type>exact</match_type>
    </custom1>
    <result>
      <profile>rules/gnome.xml</profile>
      <continue config:type="boolean">true</continue>
    </result>
    <dialog>
      <element config:type="integer">1</element>
      <dialog_nr config:type="integer">0</dialog_nr>
      <question>Gnome Desktop</question>
      <conflicts config:type="list">
        <element config:type="integer">0</element>
      </conflicts>
    </dialog>
  </rule>
  <rule>
    <custom1>
      <script>
echo -n 100
      </script>
      <match>100</match>
      <match_type>exact</match_type>
    </custom1>
    <result>
      <profile>rules/all_the_rest.xml</profile>
      <continue config:type="boolean">false</continue>
    </result>
  </rule>
```

```
</rules>
```

5.2 Classes

Classes represent configurations for groups of target systems. Unlike rules, classes need to be configured in the control file. Then classes can be assigned to target systems.

Here is an example of a class definition:

```
<classes config:type="list">
  <class>
    <class_name>TrainingRoom</class_name>
    <configuration>Software.xml</configuration>
  </class>
</classes>
```

In the example above, the file `Software.xml` must be placed in the subdirectory `classes/TrainingRoom/` It will get fetched from the same place the AutoYaST control file and rules were fetched from.

If you have multiple control files and those control files share parts, better use classes for common parts. You can also use XIncludes.

Using the configuration management system, you can define a set of classes. A class definition consists of the following variables:

- Name: class name
- Description:
- Order: order (or priority) of the class in the stack of migration

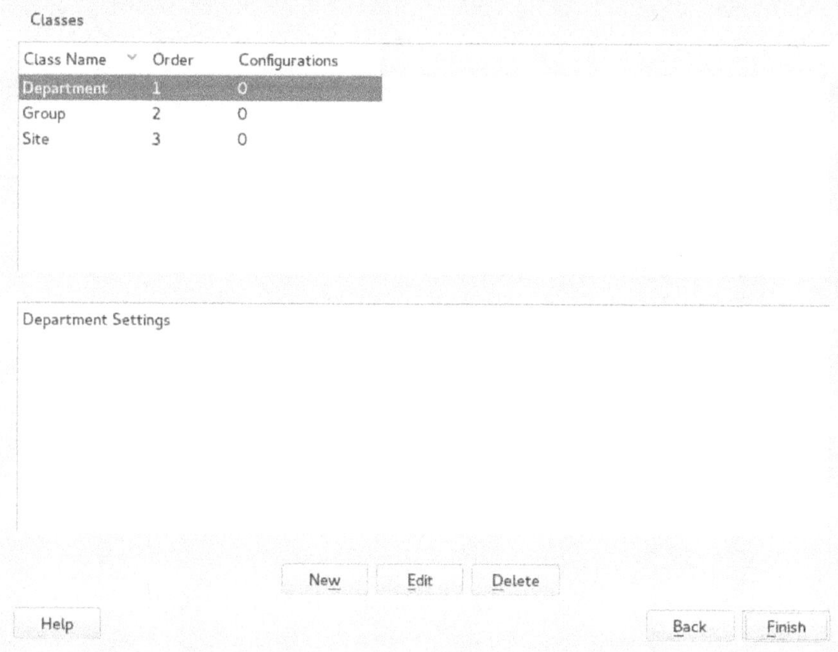

FIGURE 5.2: DEFINING CLASSES

You can create as many classes as you need, however it is recommended to keep the set of classes as small as possible to keep the configuration system concise. For example, the following sets of classes can be used:

- site: classes describing a physical location or site,
- machine: classes describing a type of machine,
- role: classes describing the function of the machine,
- group: classes describing a department or a group within a site or a location.

A file saved in a class directory can have the same syntax and format as a regular control file but represents a subset of the configuration. For example, to create a new control file for a special computer with a specific network interface, only the control file resource which controls the configuration of the network is needed. Having multiple network types, you can merge the one needed for a special type of hardware with other class files and create a new control file which suits the system being installed.

5.3 Mixing Rules and Classes

It is possible to mix rules and classes during an auto-installation session. For example you can identify a system using rules which contain class definitions in them. The process is described in the figure "*Figure A.1, "Rules Retrieval Process"*".

After retrieving the rules and merging them, the generated control file is parsed and checked for class definitions. If classes are defined, then the class files are retrieved from the original repository and a new merge process is initiated.

5.4 Merging of Rules and Classes

With classes and with rules, multiple XML files get merged into one resulting XML file. This merging process is often confusing for people, because it behaves different than one would expect. First of all it is important to note that the names of the top sections in the merged XML files need to be in alphabetical order for the merge to succeed.

For example, the following two XML parts should be merged:

```
<partitioning config:type="list">
  <drive>
    <partitions config:type="list">
      <partition>
        <filesystem config:type="symbol">swap</filesystem>
        <format config:type="boolean">true</format>
        <mount>swap</mount>
        <partition_id config:type="integer">130</partition_id>
        <size>2000mb</size>
      </partition>
      <partition>
        <filesystem config:type="symbol">xfs</filesystem>
        <partition_type>primary</partition_type>
        <size>4Gb</size>
        <mount>/data</mount>
      </partition>
    </partitions>
  </drive>
```

```
</partitioning>
```

```
<partitioning config:type="list">
  <drive>
    <initialize config:type="boolean">false</initialize>
    <partitions config:type="list">
      <partition>
        <format config:type="boolean">true</format>
        <filesystem config:type="symbol">xfs</filesystem>
        <mount>/</mount>
        <partition_id config:type="integer">131</partition_id>
        <partition_type>primary</partition_type>
        <size>max</size>
      </partition>
    </partitions>
    <use>all</use>
  </drive>
</partitioning>
```

You might expect the control file to contain 3 partitions. This is not the case. You will end up with two partitions and the first partition is a mix up of the swap and the root partition. Settings configured in both partitions, like `mount` or `size`, will be used from the second file. Settings that only exist in the first or second partition, will be copied to the merged partition too.

In this example, you do not want a second `drive`. The two drives should be merged into one. With regard to partitions, three separate ones should be defined. Using the `dont_merge` method solves the merging problem:

```
<classes config:type="list">
  <class>
    <class_name>swap</class_name>
    <configuration>largeswap.xml</configuration>
    <dont_merge config:type="list">
      <element>partition</element>
    </dont_merge>
  </class>
</classes>
```

```
<rule>
  <board_vendor>
    <match>ntel</match>
    <match_type>regex</match_type>
  </board_vendor>
  <result>
    <profile>classes/largeswap.xml</profile>
    <continue config:type="boolean">true</continue>
    <dont_merge config:type="list">
      <element>partition</element>
    </dont_merge>
  </result>
  <board_vendor>
    <match>PowerEdge [12]850</match>
    <match_type>regex</match_type>
  </board_vendor>
  <result>
    <profile>classes/smallswap.xml</profile>
    <continue config:type="boolean">true</continue>
    <dont_merge config:type="list">
      <element>partition</element>
    </dont_merge>
  </result>
</rule>
```

6 The Auto-Installation Process

6.1 Introduction

After the system has booted into an automatic installation and the control file has been retrieved, YaST configures the system according to the information provided in the control file. All configuration settings are summarized in a window that is shown by default and should be deactivated if a fully automatic installation is needed.

By the time YaST displays the summary of the configuration, YaST has only probed hardware and prepared the system for auto-installation. Nothing has been changed in the system yet. In case of any error, you can still abort the process.

A system should be automatically installable without the need to have any graphic adapter or monitor. Having a monitor attached to the client machine is nevertheless recommended so you can supervise the process and to get feedback in case of errors. Choose between the graphical and the text-based Ncurses interfaces. For headless clients, system messages can be monitored using the serial console.

6.1.1 X11 Interface (graphical)

This is the default interface while auto-installing. No special variables are required to activate it.

6.1.2 Serial console

Start installing a system using the serial console by adding the keyword `console` (for example `console=ttyS0`) to the command line of the kernel. This starts linuxrc in console mode and later YaST in serial console mode.

6.1.3 Text-based YaST Installation

This option can also be activated on the command line. To start YaST in text mode, add `textmode=1` on the command line.

Starting YaST in text mode is recommended when installing a client with less than 64 MB or when X11 should not be configured, especially on headless machines.

6.2 Choosing the Right Boot Medium

There are different methods for booting the client. The computer can boot from its network interface card (NIC) to receive the boot images via DHCP or TFTP. Alternatively a suitable kernel and initrd image can be loaded from a flash disk or a bootable DVD-ROM.

YaST will check for `autoinst.xml` in the root directory of the boot medium or the initrd upon start-up and switch to an automated installation if it was found. In case the control file is named differently or located elsewhere, specify its location on the Kernel command line with the parameter `AutoYaST=URL`.

6.2.1 Booting from a Flash Disk

For testing/rescue purposes or because the NIC does not have a PROM or PXE you can build a bootable flash disk to use with AutoYaST. Flash disks can also store the control file.

Tip: Creating a Bootable Flash Disk

To create a bootable flash disk, you need to copy either the SUSE Linux Enterprise Server iso image of DVD1 or the Mini CD iso image to the disk using the dd command (the flash disk must not be mounted, all data on the device will be erased):

```
dd if=PATH_TO_ISO_IMAGE of=USB_STORAGE_DEVICE bs=4M
```

6.2.2 Booting from DVD-ROM

You can use the original SUSE Linux Enterprise Server DVD-ROM number one in combination with other media. For example, the control file can be provided via a flash disk or a specified location on the network. Alternatively, create a customized DVD-ROM that includes the control file.

6.2.3 Booting via PXE over the Network

Booting via PXE requires a DHCP and a TFTP server in your network. The computer will then boot then without a physical medium. Refer to *Book "Deployment Guide", Chapter 13 "Remote Installation"* for instructions on how to set up the required infrastructure.

A problem you might run into if you do installation via PXE is that the installation will run into an endless loop, because after the first reboot, the machine is doing PXE boot again and restarts the installation instead of booting from hard disk for the second stage of the installation.

This problem can be solved in different ways. One way is to use an HTTP server to provide the AutoYaST control file. And, instead of a static control file, run a CGI script on the Web server that provides the control file and changes the TFTP server configuration for your target host. Then the next PXE boot of the machine will be from hard disk by default.

Another way is to use AutoYaST to upload a new PXE boot configuration for the target host via the control file:

```
<pxe>
  <pxe_localboot config:type="boolean">true</pxe_localboot>
  <pxelinux-config>
    DEFAULT linux
    LABEL linux
    localboot 0
  </pxelinux-config>
  <tftp-server>192.168.1.115</tftp-server>
  <pxelinux-dir>/pxelinux.cfg</pxelinux-dir>
  <filename>__MAC__</filename>
</pxe>
```

This entry will upload a new configuration for the target host to the TFTP server shortly before the first reboot happens. In most installations the TFTP daemon runs as user `nobody`. You need to make sure this user has write permissions to the `pxelinux.cfg` directory. You can also configure the file name that will be uploaded. If you use the "magic" `__MAC__` file name, the file name will be the MAC address of your machine like, for example `01-08-00-27-79-49-ee`. If the file name setting is missing, the IP address will be used for the file name.

If you want to do another auto-installation on the same machine, you need to remove the file from the TFTP server.

6.3 Invoking the Auto-Installation Process

6.3.1 Command Line Options

Adding the command line variable `autoyast` causes linuxrc to start in automated mode. linuxrc searches for a configuration file, which should be distinguished from the main control file in the following places:

- in the root directory of the initial RAM disk used for booting the system,
- in the root directory of the boot medium

The configuration file used by linuxrc can have the following keywords (for a detailed description of how linuxrc works and other keywords, see *Appendix B, Advanced Linuxrc Options*):

TABLE 6.1: KEYWORDS FOR LINUXRC

Keyword	Value
`autoupgrade`	Initiate an automatic upgrade using AutoYaST. Also requires the `autoyast` parameter (see *Table 6.2, "Command Line Variables for AutoYaST"* for details).
`autoyast`	Location of the control file for automatic installation, see *Table 6.2, "Command Line Variables for AutoYaST"* for details.
`gateway`	Gateway
`hostip`	When empty, client sends BOOTP request, otherwise client is configured with entered IP configuration.
`insmod`	Kernel modules to load
`install`	Location of the installation directory, for example `install=nfs://192.168.2.1/CDs/`.

Keyword	Value
`instmode`	Installation mode, for example `nfs`, `http` etc. (not needed if `install` is set).
`nameserver`	Name Server
`netdevice`	Network device to use for network setup (for BOOTP and DHCP requests)
`netmask`	Netmask
`server`	Server (NFS) to contact for source directory
`serverdir`	Directory on NFS Server
`y2confirm`	Even with <confirm>no</confirm> in the control file, the confirm proposal comes up.

These variables and keywords will bring the system up to the point where YaST can take over with the main control file. Currently, the source medium is automatically discovered, which in some cases makes it possible to initiate the auto-install process without giving any instructions to linuxrc.

The traditional linuxrc configuration file (`info`) has the function of giving the client enough information about the installation server and the location of the sources. Usually this file is not needed; it is however needed in special network environments where DHCP and BOOTP are not used or when special kernel modules need to be loaded.

All linuxrc keywords can be passed to linuxrc using the kernel command line. The command line can also be set when creating network bootable images or it can be passed to the kernel using a specially configured DHCP server in combination with Etherboot or PXE.

The command line variable `autoyast` can be used in the format described in table "*Table 6.2, "Command Line Variables for AutoYaST"*"

TABLE 6.2: COMMAND LINE VARIABLES FOR AUTOYAST

Command line variable	Description
`autoyast=default`	Default auto-installation option.

Command line variable	Description
`autoyast=file:///PATH`	Looks for control file in specified path (relative to the source root directory, for example `file:///autoinst.xml` if in the top directory of a CD-ROM and you did an installation from CD).
`autoyast=device://DEVICE/FILENAME`	Looks for control file on a storage device. Do not specify the full path to the device, but rather the device name only, for example You may also omit specifying the device and trigger AutoYaST to search all devices (`autoyast=device:///FILENAME`).
`autoyast=nfs://SERVER/PATH`	Looks for control file on an NFS server.
`autoyast=http://[user:password@]SERVER/PATH`	Retrieves the control file from a Web server using the HTTP protocol. Specifying a user name and a password is optional.
`autoyast=https://[user:password@]SERVER/PATH`	Retrieves the control file from a Web server using HTTPS. Specifying a user name and a password is optional.
`autoyast=tftp://SERVER/PATH`	Retrieve the control file via TFTP.
`autoyast=ftp://[user:password@]SERVER/PATH`	Retrieve the control file via FTP. Specifying a user name and a password is optional.
`autoyast=usb://PATH`	Retrieve the control file from USB devices (AutoYaST will search all connected USB devices).
`autoyast=relurl://PATH`	Retrieve the control file from the installation source (install=....).

Command line variable	Description
`autoyast=slp`	Query the location of the control file from an SLP server (service:autoyast:...). Optionally you may add a `description=` attribute so you can "translate" the URL into something more readable. (`autoyast=slp:/?descr=*SLES*`
`autoyast=cifs://SERVER/PATH`	Looks for control file on a CIFS server.
`autoyast=label://LABEL/PATH`	Searches for a control file on a device with the specified label

Several scenarios for auto-installation are possible using different types of infrastructure and source media. The simplest way is to use the source media (DVD number one) of SUSE Linux Enterprise Server. To initiate the auto-installation process however, the auto-installation command line variable should be entered at system boot-up and the control file should be accessible for YaST.

In a scripting context, you can use a serial console for your virtual machine, that allows you to work in text mode. Then you can pass the needed parameters from an expect script or equivalent.

The following list of scenarios explains how the control file can be supplied:

Using the Original SUSE Linux Enterprise Server DVD-ROM

When using the original DVD-ROM (DVD #1 is needed), the control file needs to be accessible via flash disk or network:

Flash Disk. Access the control file via the `autoyast=usb://PATH` option.

Network. Access the control file via the following commands: `autoyast=nfs://..`, `autoyast=ftp://..`, `autoyast=http://..`, `autoyast=https://..`, `autoyast=tftp://..`, or `autoyast=cifs://..`.

Using a Custom DVD-ROM

In this case, you can include the control file directly on the DVD-ROM. When placing it in the root directory and naming it `autoinst.xml`, it will automatically be found and used for the installation. Otherwise use `autoyast=file:///PATH` to specify the path to the control file.

When using a DVD-ROM for auto-installation, it is necessary to instruct the installer to use the DVD-ROM for installation and not try to find the installation files on the network. This can be accomplished by adding the `instmode=cd` option to the kernel command line (this can be automated done by adding the option to the `isolinux.cfg` file on the DVD).

Using a Network Installation Source

This option is the most important one because of the fact that installations of multiple machines is usually done using SLP or NFS servers and other network services like BOOTP and DHCP. The easiest way to make the control file available is to place it in the root directory of the installation source naming it `autoinst.xml`. In this case it will automatically be found and used for the installation. The control file can also reside in the following places:

Flash Disk. Access the control file via the `autoyast=usb://PATH` option.

Network. Access the control file via the following commands: `autoyast=nfs://..`, `autoyast=ftp://..`, `autoyast=http://..`, `autoyast=https://..`, `autoyast=tftp://..`, or `autoyast=cifs://..`.

Note: Disabling Network and DHCP

To disable the network during installations where it is not needed or unavailable, for example when auto-installing from DVD-ROMs, use the linuxrc option `netsetup=0` to disable the network setup.

If `autoyast=default` is defined, YaST will look for a file named `autoinst.xml` in the following three places:

1. the root directory of the flash disk,
2. the root directory of the installation medium,
3. the root directory of the initial RAM disk used to boot the system.

With all AutoYaST invocation options, excluding `default`, it is possible to specify the location of the control file in the following ways:

1. Specify the exact location of the control file:

   ```
   autoyast=http://192.168.1.1/control-files/client01.xml
   ```

2. Specify a directory where several control files are located:

   ```
   autoyast=http://192.168.1.1/control-files/
   ```

   In this case the relevant control file is retrieved using the hex digit representation of the IP as described below.

If only the path prefix variable is defined, YaST will fetch the control file from the specified location in the following way:

1. First, it will search for the control file using its own IP address in uppercase hexadecimal, for example `192.0.2.91 -> C000025B`.
2. If this file is not found, YaST will remove one hex digit and try again. This action is repeated until the file with the correct name is found. Ultimately, it will try looking for a file with the MAC address of the client as the file name (mac should have the following syntax: `0080C8F6484C`) and if not found a file named `default` (in lowercase).

As an example, for 192.0.2.91, the HTTP client will try:

```
C000025B
C000025
C00002
C0000
C000
C00
C0
C
0080C8F6484C
default
```

in that order.

To determine the hex representation of the IP address of the client, use the utility called **/usr/bin/gethostip** available with the `syslinux` package.

EXAMPLE 6.1: DETERMINE HEX CODE FOR AN IP ADDRESS

```
# /usr/bin/gethostip 10.10.0.1
10.10.0.1 10.10.0.1 0A0A0001
```

6.3.2 Auto-installing a Single System

The easiest way to auto-install a system without any network connection is to use the original SUSE Linux Enterprise Server DVD-ROMs and a flash disk. You do not need to set up an installation server nor the network environment.

Create the control file and name it `autoinst.xml`. Copy the file `autoinst.xml` to the flash disk.

6.3.3 Combining the linuxrc `info` file with the AutoYaST control file

If you choose to pass information to linuxrc using the `info` file, it is possible to integrate the keywords in the XML control file. In this case the file needs to be accessible to linuxrc and needs to be named `info`.

Linuxrc will look for a string (`start_linuxrc_conf` in the control file which represents the beginning of the file. If it is found, it will parse the content starting from that string and will finish when the string `end_linuxrc_conf` is found. The options are stored in the control file in the following way:

EXAMPLE 6.2: LINUXRC OPTIONS IN THE CONTROL FILE

```
....
  <install>
....
    <init>
      <info_file>
<![CDATA[
```

```
#
# Do not remove the following line:
# start_linuxrc_conf
#
install: nfs://192.168.1.1/CDs/full-i386
textmode: 1
autoyast: file:///info

# end_linuxrc_conf
# Do not remove the above comment
#
]]>

      </info_file>
    </init>
......
  </install>
....
```

Note that the `autoyast` keyword must point to the same file. If it is on a flash disk, then the option `usb:///` needs to be used. If the `info` file is stored in the initial RAM disk, the `file://` option needs to be used.

6.4 System Configuration

The system configuration during auto-installation is the most important part of the whole process. As you have seen in the previous chapters, almost anything can be configured automatically on the target system. In addition to the pre-defined directives, you can always use post-scripts to change other things in the system. Additionally you can change any system variables, and if required, copy complete configuration files into the target system.

6.4.1 Post-Install and System Configuration

The post-installation and system configuration are initiated directly after the last package is installed on the target system and continue after the system has booted for the first time.

Before the system is booted for the first time, AutoYaST writes all data collected during installation and writes the boot loader in the specified location. In addition to these regular tasks, AutoYaST executes the chroot-scripts as specified in the control file. Note that these scripts are executed while the system is not yet mounted.

If a different kernel than the default is installed, a hard reboot will be required. A hard reboot can also be forced during auto-installation, independent of the installed kernel. Use the `reboot` property of the `general` resource (see General Options).

6.4.2 System Customization

Most of the system customization is done in the second stage of the installation. If you require customization that cannot be done using AutoYaST resources, use post-install scripts for further modifications.

You can define an unlimited number of custom scripts in the control file, either by editing the control file or by using the configuration system.

A Handling Rules

The following figure illustrates how rules are handled and the processes of retrieval and merge.

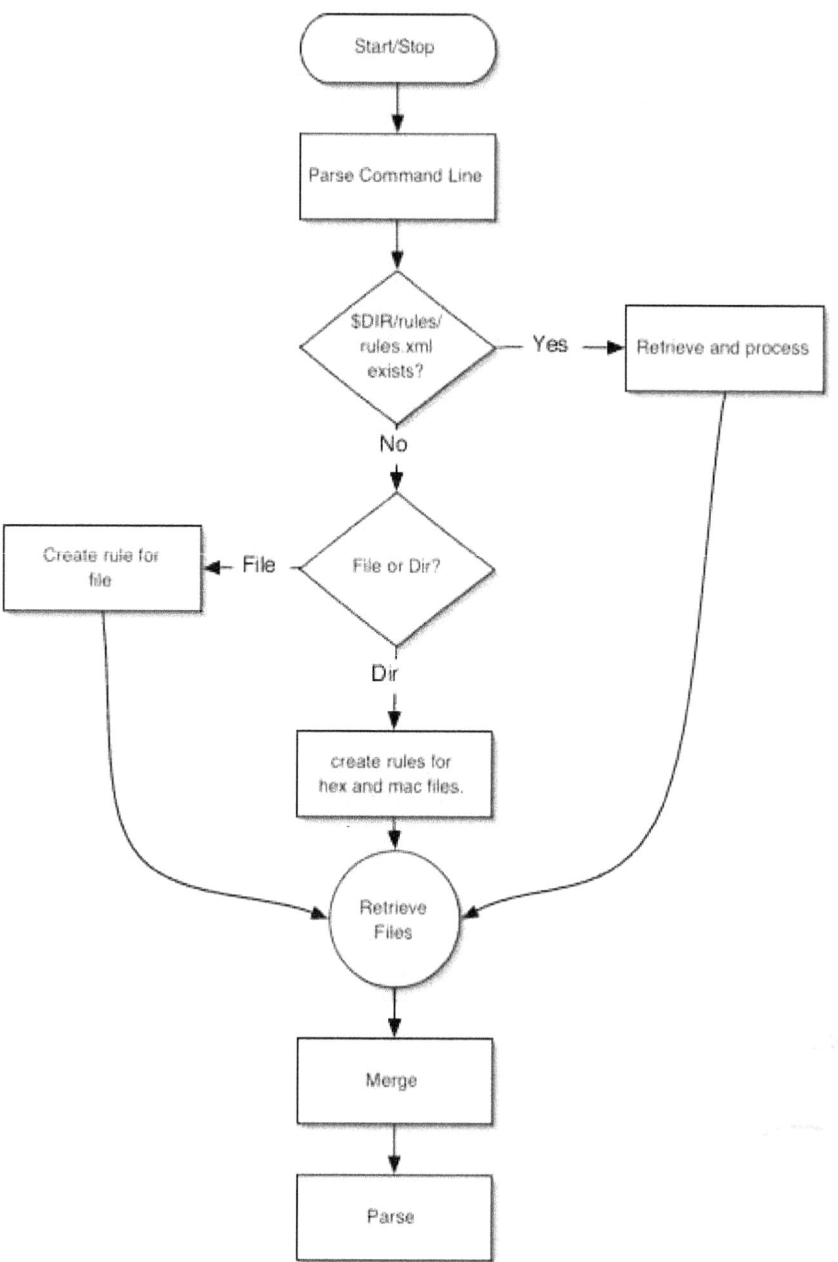

FIGURE A.1: RULES RETRIEVAL PROCESS

B Advanced Linuxrc Options

Linuxrc is a program used for setting up the kernel for installation purposes. It allows the user to load modules, start an installed system, a rescue system or an installation via YaST.

Linuxrc is designed to be as small as possible. Therefore, all needed programs are linked directly into one binary. So there is no need for shared libraries in the initdisk.

Note: Running Linuxrc on an Installed System

If you run Linuxrc on an installed system, it will work slightly differently so as not to destroy your installation. As a consequence you cannot test all features this way.

B.1 Passing parameters to Linuxrc

Unless Linuxrc is in manual mode, it will look for an `info` file in these locations: first `/info` on the flash disk and if that does not exist, for `/info` in the initrd. After that it parses the kernel command line for parameters. You may change the `info` file Linuxrc reads by setting the `info` command line parameter. If you do not want Linuxrc to read the kernel command line (for example because you need to specify a kernel parameter that Linuxrc recognizes as well), use `linuxrc=nocmdline`.

Linuxrc will always look for and parse a file `/linuxrc.config`. Use this file to change default values if you need to. In general, it is better to use the `info` file instead. Note that `/linuxrc.config` is read before any `info` file, even in manual mode.

B.2 info file format

Lines starting with `#` are comments, valid entries are of the form:

```
key: value
```

Note that `value` extends to the end of the line and therefore may contain spaces. `key` is matched case-insensitive.

You can use the same key-value pairs on the kernel command line using the syntax `key=value`. Lines that do not have the form described above are ignored.

The table below lists Valid keys. The given values are only examples.

TABLE B.1: ADVANCED LINUXRC KEYWORDS

Keyword/Value	Description
AddSwap: 0|3|/dev/sda5	If 0, never ask for swap; if the argument is a positive number `n`, activate the `n`'th swap partition; if the argument is a partition name, activate this swap partition
AutoYaST: ftp://autoyastfile	Location of the auto installation file; activates auto installation mode
BOOTPTimeout: 10	10 seconds timeout for BOOTP requests
BOOTPWait: 5	Sleep 5 seconds between network activation and starting bootp
DHCPTimeout: 60	60 seconds timeout for DHCP requests
Display: Color|Mono|Alt	Set the menu color scheme
DHCP: 0|1	Start the DHCP daemon now>, but see `UseDHCP`
Domain: example.com	Set domain name (used for name server lookups)
Exec: command	Run *command*
ForceInsmod: 0|1	Use `-f` option when running **`insmod`**
ForceRootimage: 0|1	Load the installation system into RAM disk
Gateway: 10.10.0.1	Gateway
HostIP: 10.10.0.2	The client ip address
Insmod: module params	Load this module

Keyword/Value	Description
Install: nfs://*SERVER*/install/8.0-i386	Install via NFS from *SERVER* (note: you can specify user name, password etc. in the URL, too)
InstallDir: /suse/inst-sys	Installation system
InstMode: cd|hd|nfs|smb|ftp|http|tftp	Set installation mode
Keytable: de-lat1-nd	Load this key table
Language: de_DE	Set the language
Loghost: 10.10.0.22	Enable remove logging via syslog
Manual: 0|1	Start Linuxrc in manual mode
MemLoadImage: 50000	Load installation system into RAM disk if free memory is above 50000 KB
MemLimit: 10000	Ask for swap if free memory drops below 10000 KB
MemModules: 20000	Delete all modules before starting YaST if free memory is below 20000 KB
MemYaST: 20000	Run YaST in text mode if free memory is below 20000 KB
MemYaSTText: 10000	Ask for swap before starting YaST if free memory is below 10000 KB
Nameserver: 10.10.0.1	Name Server
Netdevice: eth0	Network interface to use
Netmask: 255.255.0.0	Network mask
NoPCMCIA: 0|1	Do not start card manager

Keyword/Value	**Description**
Partition: hda1	Partition with install sources for hard disk install
Password: password	Set password (for example for an FTP installation)
Proxy: 10.10.0.1	Proxy (either FTP or HTTP)
ProxyPort: 10.10.0.1	Proxy port
Rescue: 1|nfs://server/dir	Load rescue system; the URL variant specifies the location of the rescue image explicitly
RescueImage: /suse/images/rescue	Rescue system image
RootImage: /suse/images/root	Installation system image
Server: 10.10.0.1	Installation server address
Serverdir: /install/8.0-i386	Base directory of the installation sources
ssh.password: password	Sets SSH server password (this will not be the final root password!)
Textmode: 0|1	Start YaST in text mode
TFTPTimeout: 10	10 seconds timeout for TFTP connection
USBWait: 4	Wait 4 seconds after loading USB modules
UseDHCP: 0|1	Use DHCP instead of BOOTP (DHCP is default)
Username: name	Set user name (for example for an FTP installation)
ssh: 0|1	Setup SSH server

Keyword/Value	Description
vlan: `VLANID`	Set a `VLANID` to enable 802.1q tagged VLAN support
vnc: 0|1	Setup VNC server
VNCPassword: password	Sets VNC server password
WorkDomain: domain	Set work domain for SMB install
y2confirm	Overrides the confirm parameter in a control file and requests confirmation of installation proposal

B.3 Advanced Network Setup

The `netsetup` keyword allows advanced network configurations and enables dialogs to set up the network where required.

- netsetup=1
  the normal network setup questions
- netsetup=xxx,yyy
  only xxx and yyy
- netsetup= +xxx,-yyy
  default, additionally xxx, but not yyy

`netsetup` can have the following values: `dhcp`, `hostip`, `gateway`, `netmask`, `name server`. `nameserverN` asks for N name servers (max. 4).

For example, the following can be entered on the command line:

```
netsetup=-dhcp,+nameserver3
```

C Documentation Updates

This chapter lists content changes for this document.

This manual was updated on the following dates:

- *Section C.1, "December 2015 ((Initial Release of SUSE Linux Enterprise Server 12 SP1)"*
- *Section C.2, "February 2015 (Documentation Maintenance Update)"*
- *Section C.3, "October 2014 (Initial Release of SUSE Linux Enterprise Server 12)"*

C.1 December 2015 ((Initial Release of SUSE Linux Enterprise Server 12 SP1)

General

- *Book "Subscription Management Tool for SLES 12 SP1"* is now part of the documentation for SUSE Linux Enterprise Server.
- Add-ons provided by SUSE have been renamed to modules and extensions. The manuals have been updated to reflect this change.
- Numerous small fixes and additions to the documentation, based on technical feedback.
- The registration service has been changed from Novell Customer Center to SUSE Customer Center.
- In YaST, you will now reach *Network Settings* via the *System* group. *Network Devices* is gone (https://bugzilla.suse.com/show_bug.cgi?id=867809).

-

Bugfixes

- Added a note on installation errors when trying to remove a package that is part of a pattern (https://bugzilla.suse.com/show_bug.cgi?id=928074).

C.2 February 2015 (Documentation Maintenance Update)

Bugfixes

- AutoYaST documentation is missing most tag and attributes description (https://bugzilla.suse.com/show_bug.cgi?id=883393).
- AutoYaST documentation for LVM groups is wrong (https://bugzilla.suse.com/show_bug.cgi?id=906362).

C.3 October 2014 (Initial Release of SUSE Linux Enterprise Server 12)

General

- Removed all KDE documentation and references because KDE is no longer shipped.
- Removed all references to SuSEconfig, which is no longer supported (Fate #100011).
- Move from System V init to systemd (Fate #310421). Updated affected parts of the documentation.
- YaST Runlevel Editor has changed to Services Manager (Fate #312568). Updated affected parts of the documentation.
- Removed all references to ISDN support, as ISDN support has been removed (Fate #314594).
- Removed all references to the YaST DSL module as it is no longer shipped (Fate #316264).

- Removed all references to the YaST Modem module as it is no longer shipped (Fate #316264).
- Btrfs has become the default file system for the root partition (Fate #315901). Updated affected parts of the documentation.
- The **dmesg** now provides human-readable time stamps in `ctime()` -like format (Fate #316056). Updated affected parts of the documentation.
- syslog and syslog-ng have been replaced by rsyslog (Fate #316175). Updated affected parts of the documentation.
- MariaDB is now shipped as the relational database instead of MySQL (Fate #313595). Updated affected parts of the documentation.
- SUSE-related products are no longer available from http://download.novell.com but from http://download.suse.com. Adjusted links accordingly.
- Novell Customer Center has been replaced with SUSE Customer Center. Updated affected parts of the documentation.
- `/var/run` is mounted as tmpfs (Fate #303793). Updated affected parts of the documentation.
- The following architectures are no longer supported: Itanium and x86. Updated affected parts of the documentation.
- The traditional method for setting up the network with `ifconfig` has been replaced by `wicked`. Updated affected parts of the documentation.
- A lot of networking commands are deprecated and have been replaced by newer commands (usually **ip**). Updated affected parts of the documentation.

  arp: **ip neighbor**
  ifconfig: **ip addr**, **ip link**
  iptunnel: **ip tunnel**
  iwconfig: **iw**
  nameif: **ip link**, **ifrename**
  netstat: **ss**, **ip route**, **ip -s link**, **ip maddr**
  route: **ip route**
- Numerous small fixes and additions to the documentation, based on technical feedback.

Chapter 1, Introduction

- Added a note on how to deactivate the second stage of the installation to *Section 1.2, "Overview and Concept"*.

Chapter 4, Configuration and Installation Options

- Added a tip on how to enable multipath for the installation to *Section 4.1, "General Options"* (Fate #316278).
- Added *Section 4.3, "System Registration and Extension Selection"*.
- Updated *Section 4.4, "The Boot Loader"* to reflect the changes that came with GRUB 2.
- Updated the ***Detailed Automated Partitioning*** example in *Section 4.5.4, "Automated Partitioning"*.
- Replaced the ***LDAP Client*** chapter with *Section 4.18, "Authentication Client"* explaining the new authentication setup procedure with SSSD (Fate #316089).
- Added a tip on how to use ldaps:// to *Section 4.18, "Authentication Client"* (Fate #316086).
- Adjusted *Section 4.35.1, "Printer"* to reflect the new AutoYaST syntax for setting up a printer.

Bugfixes

- *Section 4.35.1, "Printer"*: AutoYaST printer config: Since CUPS > 1.6 now cupsd.conf plus cups-files.conf (https://bugzilla.suse.com/show_bug.cgi?id=871847).
- *Chapter 5, Rules and Classes*: autoyast rules - some attributes are accepted even does not match exactly (https://bugzilla.suse.com/show_bug.cgi?id=872690).
- *Section 5.1.6, "Predefined System Attributes"*: ayast_probe - error message "The storage subsystem is locked by the application y2base..." (https://bugzilla.suse.com/show_bug.cgi?id=872551).
- *Section 6.3, "Invoking the Auto-Installation Process"*: AutoYast does not support 802.1q tagged VLAN (https://bugzilla.suse.com/show_bug.cgi?id=852316).

D GNU Licenses

This appendix contains the GNU Free Documentation License version 1.2.

GNU Free Documentation License

0. PREAMBLE

The purpose of this License is to make a manual, textbook, or other functional and useful document "free" in the sense of freedom: to assure everyone the effective freedom to copy and redistribute it, with or without modifying it, either commercially or non-commercially. Secondarily, this License preserves for the author and publisher a way to get credit for their work, while not being considered responsible for modifications made by others.

This License is a kind of "copyleft", which means that derivative works of the document must themselves be free in the same sense. It complements the GNU General Public License, which is a copyleft license designed for free software.

We have designed this License to use it for manuals for free software, because free software needs free documentation: a free program should come with manuals providing the same freedoms that the software does. But this License is not limited to software manuals; it can be used for any textual work, regardless of subject matter or whether it is published as a printed book. We recommend this License principally for works whose purpose is instruction or reference.

1. APPLICABILITY AND DEFINITIONS

This License applies to any manual or other work, in any medium, that contains a notice placed by the copyright holder saying it can be distributed under the terms of this License. Such a notice grants a world-wide, royalty-free license, unlimited in duration, to use that work under the conditions stated herein. The "Document", below, refers to any such manual or work. Any member of the public is a licensee, and is addressed as "you". You accept the license if you copy, modify or distribute the work in a way requiring permission under copyright law.

A "Modified Version" of the Document means any work containing the Document or a portion of it, either copied verbatim, or with modifications and/or translated into another language.

A "Secondary Section" is a named appendix or a front-matter section of the Document that deals exclusively with the relationship of the publishers or authors of the Document to the Document's overall subject (or to related matters) and contains nothing that could fall directly within that overall subject. (Thus, if the Document is in part a textbook of mathematics, a Secondary Section may not explain any mathematics.) The relationship could be a matter of historical connection with the subject or with related matters, or of legal, commercial, philosophical, ethical or political position regarding them.

The "Invariant Sections" are certain Secondary Sections whose titles are designated, as being those of Invariant Sections, in the notice that says that the Document is released under this License. If a section does not fit the above definition of Secondary then it is not allowed to be designated as Invariant. The Document may contain zero Invariant Sections. If the Document does not identify any Invariant Sections then there are none.

The "Cover Texts" are certain short passages of text that are listed, as Front-Cover Texts or Back-Cover Texts, in the notice that says that the Document is released under this License. A Front-Cover Text may be at most 5 words, and a Back-Cover Text may be at most 25 words.

A "Transparent" copy of the Document means a machine-readable copy, represented in a format whose specification is available to the general public, that is suitable for revising the document straightforwardly with generic text editors or (for images composed of pixels) generic paint programs or (for drawings) some widely available drawing editor, and that is suitable for input to text formatters or for automatic translation to a variety of formats suitable for input to text formatters. A copy made in an otherwise Transparent file format whose markup, or absence of markup, has been arranged to thwart or discourage subsequent modification by readers is not Transparent. An image format is not Transparent if used for any substantial amount of text. A copy that is not "Transparent" is called "Opaque".

Examples of suitable formats for Transparent copies include plain ASCII without markup, Texinfo input format, LaTeX input format, SGML or XML using a publicly available DTD, and standard-conforming simple HTML, PostScript or PDF designed for human modification. Examples of transparent image formats include PNG, XCF and JPG. Opaque formats include proprietary formats that can be read and edited only by proprietary word processors, SGML or XML for which the DTD and/or processing tools are not generally available, and the machine-generated HTML, PostScript or PDF produced by some word processors for output purposes only.

The "Title Page" means, for a printed book, the title page itself, plus such following pages as are needed to hold, legibly, the material this License requires to appear in the title page. For works in formats which do not have any title page as such, "Title Page" means the text near the most prominent appearance of the work's title, preceding the beginning of the body of the text.

A section "Entitled XYZ" means a named subunit of the Document whose title either is precisely XYZ or contains XYZ in parentheses following text that translates XYZ in another language. (Here XYZ stands for a specific section name mentioned below, such as "Acknowledgements", "Dedications", "Endorsements", or "History".) To "Preserve the Title" of such a section when you modify the Document means that it remains a section "Entitled XYZ" according to this definition.

The Document may include Warranty Disclaimers next to the notice which states that this License applies to the Document. These Warranty Disclaimers are considered to be included by reference in this License, but only as regards disclaiming warranties: any other implication that these Warranty Disclaimers may have is void and has no effect on the meaning of this License.

2. VERBATIM COPYING

You may copy and distribute the Document in any medium, either commercially or noncommercially, provided that this License, the copyright notices, and the license notice saying this License applies to the Document are reproduced in all copies, and that you add no other conditions whatsoever to those of this License. You may not use technical measures to obstruct or control the reading or further copying of the copies you make or distribute. However, you may accept compensation in exchange for copies. If you distribute a large enough number of copies you must also follow the conditions in section 3.

You may also lend copies, under the same conditions stated above, and you may publicly display copies.

3. COPYING IN QUANTITY

If you publish printed copies (or copies in media that commonly have printed covers) of the Document, numbering more than 100, and the Document's license notice requires Cover Texts, you must enclose the copies in covers that carry, clearly and legibly, all these Cover Texts: Front-Cover Texts on the front cover, and Back-Cover Texts on the back cover. Both covers must also clearly and legibly identify you as the publisher of these copies. The front cover must present the full title with all words of the title equally prominent and visible. You may add other material on the covers in addition. Copying with changes limited to the covers, as long as they preserve the title of the Document and satisfy these conditions, can be treated as verbatim copying in other respects.

If the required texts for either cover are too voluminous to fit legibly, you should put the first ones listed (as many as fit reasonably) on the actual cover, and continue the rest onto adjacent pages.

If you publish or distribute Opaque copies of the Document numbering more than 100, you must either include a machine-readable Transparent copy along with each Opaque copy, or state in or with each Opaque copy a computer-network location from which the general network-using public has access to download using public-standard network protocols a complete Transparent copy of the Document, free of added material. If you use the latter option, you must take reasonably prudent steps, when you begin distribution of Opaque copies in quantity, to ensure that this Transparent copy will remain thus accessible at the stated location until at least one year after the last time you distribute an Opaque copy (directly or through your agents or retailers) of that edition to the public.

It is requested, but not required, that you contact the authors of the Document well before redistributing any large number of copies, to give them a chance to provide you with an updated version of the Document.

4. MODIFICATIONS

You may copy and distribute a Modified Version of the Document under the conditions of sections 2 and 3 above, provided that you release the Modified Version under precisely this License, with the Modified Version filling the role of the Document, thus licensing distribution and modification of the Modified Version to whoever possesses a copy of it. In addition, you must do these things in the Modified Version:

A. Use in the Title Page (and on the covers, if any) a title distinct from that of the Document, and from those of previous versions (which should, if there were any, be listed in the History section of the Document). You may use the same title as a previous version if the original publisher of that version gives permission.

B. List on the Title Page, as authors, one or more persons or entities responsible for authorship of the modifications in the Modified Version, together with at least five of the principal authors of the Document (all of its principal authors, if it has fewer than five), unless they release you from this requirement.

C. State on the Title page the name of the publisher of the Modified Version, as the publisher.

D. Preserve all the copyright notices of the Document.

E. Add an appropriate copyright notice for your modifications adjacent to the other copyright notices.

F. Include, immediately after the copyright notices, a license notice giving the public permission to use the Modified Version under the terms of this License, in the form shown in the Addendum below.

G. Preserve in that license notice the full lists of Invariant Sections and required Cover Texts given in the Document's license notice.

H. Include an unaltered copy of this License.

I. Preserve the section Entitled "History", Preserve its Title, and add to it an item stating at least the title, year, new authors, and publisher of the Modified Version as given on the Title Page. If there is no section Entitled "History" in the Document, create one stating the title, year, authors, and publisher of the Document as given on its Title Page, then add an item describing the Modified Version as stated in the previous sentence.

J. Preserve the network location, if any, given in the Document for public access to a Transparent copy of the Document, and likewise the network locations given in the Document for previous versions it was based on. These may be placed in the "History" section. You may omit a network location for a work that was published at least four years before the Document itself, or if the original publisher of the version it refers to gives permission.

K. For any section Entitled "Acknowledgements" or "Dedications", Preserve the Title of the section, and preserve in the section all the substance and tone of each of the contributor acknowledgements and/or dedications given therein.

L. Preserve all the Invariant Sections of the Document, unaltered in their text and in their titles. Section numbers or the equivalent are not considered part of the section titles.

M. Delete any section Entitled "Endorsements". Such a section may not be included in the Modified Version.

N. Do not retitle any existing section to be Entitled "Endorsements" or to conflict in title with any Invariant Section.

O. Preserve any Warranty Disclaimers.

If the Modified Version includes new front-matter sections or appendices that qualify as Secondary Sections and contain no material copied from the Document, you may at your option designate some or all of these sections as invariant. To do this, add their titles to the list of Invariant Sections in the Modified Version's license notice. These titles must be distinct from any other section titles.

You may add a section Entitled "Endorsements", provided it contains nothing but endorsements of your Modified Version by various parties--for example, statements of peer review or that the text has been approved by an organization as the authoritative definition of a standard.

You may add a passage of up to five words as a Front-Cover Text, and a passage of up to 25 words as a Back-Cover Text, to the end of the list of Cover Texts in the Modified Version. Only one passage of Front-Cover Text and one of Back-Cover Text may be added by (or through arrangements made by) any one entity. If the Document already includes a cover text for the same cover, previously added by you or by arrangement made by the same entity you are acting on behalf of, you may not add another; but you may replace the old one, on explicit permission from the previous publisher that added the old one.

The author(s) and publisher(s) of the Document do not by this License give permission to use their names for publicity for or to assert or imply endorsement of any Modified Version.

5. COMBINING DOCUMENTS

You may combine the Document with other documents released under this License, under the terms defined in section 4 above for modified versions, provided that you include in the combination all of the Invariant Sections of all of the original documents, unmodified, and list them all as Invariant Sections of your combined work in its license notice, and that you preserve all their Warranty Disclaimers.

The combined work need only contain one copy of this License, and multiple identical Invariant Sections may be replaced with a single copy. If there are multiple Invariant Sections with the same name but different contents, make the title of each such section unique by adding at the end of it, in parentheses, the name of the original author or publisher of that section if known, or else a unique number. Make the same adjustment to the section titles in the list of Invariant Sections in the license notice of the combined work.

In the combination, you must combine any sections Entitled "History" in the various original documents, forming one section Entitled "History"; likewise combine any sections Entitled "Acknowledgements", and any sections Entitled "Dedications". You must delete all sections Entitled "Endorsements".

6. COLLECTIONS OF DOCUMENTS

You may make a collection consisting of the Document and other documents released under this License, and replace the individual copies of this License in the various documents with a single copy that is included in the collection, provided that you follow the rules of this License for verbatim copying of each of the documents in all other respects.

You may extract a single document from such a collection, and distribute it individually under this License, provided you insert a copy of this License into the extracted document, and follow this License in all other respects regarding verbatim copying of that document.

7. AGGREGATION WITH INDEPENDENT WORKS

A compilation of the Document or its derivatives with other separate and independent documents or works, in or on a volume of a storage or distribution medium, is called an "aggregate" if the copyright resulting from the compilation is not used to limit the legal rights of the compilation's users beyond what the individual works permit. When the Document is included in an aggregate, this License does not apply to the other works in the aggregate which are not themselves derivative works of the Document.

If the Cover Text requirement of section 3 is applicable to these copies of the Document, then if the Document is less than one half of the entire aggregate, the Document's Cover Texts may be placed on covers that bracket the Document within the aggregate, or the electronic equivalent of covers if the Document is in electronic form. Otherwise they must appear on printed covers that bracket the whole aggregate.

8. TRANSLATION

Translation is considered a kind of modification, so you may distribute translations of the Document under the terms of section 4. Replacing Invariant Sections with translations requires special permission from their copyright holders, but you may include translations of some or all Invariant Sections in addition to the original versions of these Invariant Sections. You may include a translation of this License, and all the license notices in the Document, and any Warranty Disclaimers, provided that you also include the original English version of this License and the original versions of those notices and disclaimers. In case of a disagreement between the translation and the original version of this License or a notice or disclaimer, the original version will prevail.

If a section in the Document is Entitled "Acknowledgements", "Dedications", or "History", the requirement (section 4) to Preserve its Title (section 1) will typically require changing the actual title.

9. TERMINATION

You may not copy, modify, sublicense, or distribute the Document except as expressly provided for under this License. Any other attempt to copy, modify, sublicense or distribute the Document is void, and will automatically terminate your rights under this License. However, parties who have received copies, or rights, from you under this License will not have their licenses terminated so long as such parties remain in full compliance.

10. FUTURE REVISIONS OF THIS LICENSE

The Free Software Foundation may publish new, revised versions of the GNU Free Documentation License from time to time. Such new versions will be similar in spirit to the present version, but may differ in detail to address new problems or concerns. See http://www.gnu.org/copyleft/.

Each version of the License is given a distinguishing version number. If the Document specifies that a particular numbered version of this License "or any later version" applies to it, you have the option of following the terms and conditions either of that specified version or of any later version that has been published (not as a draft) by the Free Software Foundation. If the Document does not specify a version number of this License, you may choose any version ever published (not as a draft) by the Free Software Foundation.

ADDENDUM: How to use this License for your documents

```
Copyright (c) YEAR YOUR NAME.

Permission is granted to copy, distribute and/or modify this document

under the terms of the GNU Free Documentation License, Version 1.2

or any later version published by the Free Software Foundation;

with no Invariant Sections, no Front-Cover Texts, and no Back-Cover

 Texts.

A copy of the license is included in the section entitled “GNU

Free Documentation License”.
```

If you have Invariant Sections, Front-Cover Texts and Back-Cover Texts, replace the “with...Texts.” line with this:

```
with the Invariant Sections being LIST THEIR TITLES, with the

Front-Cover Texts being LIST, and with the Back-Cover Texts being LIST.
```

If you have Invariant Sections without Cover Texts, or some other combination of the three, merge those two alternatives to suit the situation.

If your document contains nontrivial examples of program code, we recommend releasing these examples in parallel under your choice of free software license, such as the GNU General Public License, to permit their use in free software.

www.ingramcontent.com/pod-product-compliance
Lightning Source LLC
LaVergne TN
LVHW060139070326
832902LV00018B/2860

* 9 7 8 9 8 8 8 4 0 6 5 5 5 *